History of the Jews

A Captivating Guide to Jewish History, Starting from the Ancient Israelites through Roman Rule to World War 2

Free Bonus from Captivating History
(Available for a Limited time)

Hi History Lovers!

Now you have a chance to join our exclusive history list so you can get your first history ebook for free as well as discounts and a potential to get more history books for free! Simply visit the link below to join.

Captivatinghistory.com/ebook

Also, make sure to follow us on Facebook, Twitter and Youtube by searching for Captivating History.

Contents

Introduction: In the Beginning...

Peoples and cultures from all over the world and throughout history have produced their own unique origin story. The origin story of the Jews and mankind in general can be found in the biblical Book of Genesis. While not everyone believes in the veracity of the Bible, billions of Jews, Christians, and Muslims, who hold the narrative dear to their own respective religions, would have to disagree.

According to Genesis (or as it is called in Hebrew, "Bereshit," which literally means "in the beginning"), before creation, the earth was "formless and empty" and "darkness was over the surface of the deep." The Book of Genesis then goes on to describe how God brought life to the earth, creating all manner of plants and animals, before finally designing the greatest showpiece of his creation— humanity itself.

For those who interpret the scriptures literally, this was the actual beginning of Jewish history. Of course, the more skeptical and cynical among us would most certainly beg to differ. At any rate, even though the Book of Genesis offers up one of the most famous creation stories of all time, the creation of the Book of Genesis itself can be traced back, not to the dawn of time but rather just a few thousand years ago. It is believed to have been written by a man named Moses.

Moses, in fact, is credited with writing the first five books of the Bible/Torah. It is believed that Moses compiled the Torah around 1445 BCE while the nation of Israel was making their exodus from Egypt (the Book of Exodus is actually the book right after Genesis). Regardless of when it was written, and regardless of whether anyone believes it or not, the Book of Genesis attempts to tell the story of the beginning of Jewish history.

Moses, or whoever may have chronicled the events, had to cast their mind backward in time to tell us what happened. After the general creation story, the Book of Genesis follows a specific lineage of people, which ultimately leads up to the great biblical patriarch, Abraham. It is Abraham who is identified as the founding father of Judaism as a religion.

Abraham was from an ancient city in the Middle East called "Ur." The city of Ur is located in modern-day Iraq, near the city of Nasiriyah. According to the narrative of Genesis, most of the people in this region were polytheists, meaning they believed in many gods. It is revealed to Abraham that there is only one God. From this revelation, he developed the first strains of the monotheistic religion that would eventually become Judaism.

Ironically enough, it is said that Abraham's own father, Terah, made a living by making and selling stone idols. Regardless of his father's influence, Abraham would grow up to very much live by the motto of "It is not man who makes God but God who makes man." Abraham, who no longer believed that new gods could be simply carved up in stone on demand, began revealing his newfound belief in one supreme deity to all who would listen to him.

Along with this newfound monotheistic belief system, Abraham was given a mission to travel to the land of Canaan (modern-day Israel/Palestine). According to Genesis 12: 2-3, God told Abraham, "I will make you into a great nation, and I will bless you; I will make your name great, and you will be a blessing. I will bless those who bless you, and whoever curses you I will curse; and all peoples on earth will be blessed through you."

It's certainly a pretty heady thing to tell a man that "all peoples on Earth will be blessed" *through him*. But this covenant is said to have represented much more than just Abraham. Many theologians have come to interpret Abraham as being a symbolic double for the nation of Israel itself. At any rate, Abraham answered this divine summons, and he took his family along with him, which, at that time, consisted of his wife, Sarah, and the son of his brother, Lot.

All seemed to be well in the land of Canaan until a devastating famine struck. The famine caused Abraham to take his wife and his brother's son and venture south of Canaan into the land of Egypt. Abraham managed to bring quite a bit of wealth back with him, and for a time, he and his family did quite well. However, according to the scripture, drama unfolded when Sarah, who, at the time, was unable to bear any children, convinced her husband Abraham to sleep with her "handmaiden" Hagar so that he could have a child through her.

According to scripture, Hagar gave birth to Ishmael. Problems later arose when Sarah and Abraham managed to have a child of their own, whom they named Isaac. As she had her own child to raise, Sarah began to resent Hagar and Ishmael, and she essentially drove them off. An angel intervened to help shepherd Hagar and Ishmael through the desert and ensure their survival. Coincidentally enough, Arabs have, for a long time, traced their lineage from Ishmael.

The next major episode in Abraham's life was when God decided to "test" Abraham by ordering him to sacrifice his one and only begotten son, Isaac. Abraham had no idea why God would do such a thing, but he knew God's will had a purpose. So, with great sadness, he obeyed. According to Genesis, it was right when he was about to drive the knife into his own son that an angel intervened, saying that the whole thing was just a test of his faith.

Christians would later point to this part of the Bible and draw parallels with the notion that God was willing to sacrifice his own son, Jesus, on the cross. Others have pointed out that this might have been an object lesson for Abraham to show him that the God of Israel would not demand human sacrifices, unlike the gods the other inhabitants of Canaan worshiped, with whom human sacrifice was thought to be quite common.

At any rate, it was through Isaac that the lineage of what would become the nation of Israel progressed. Isaac was the father of Jacob, who would later take on the name of Israel. From Jacob came twelve sons, from which the "twelve tribes of Israel" are derived. But the next important person in this narrative would have to be Joseph, who, through his brothers' jealousy and trickery, was sold into slavery in Egypt.

According to scripture, although Joseph's fate initially seemed rather bleak, his fortune turned around considerably. He went from being a slave to a high-ranking member of the pharaoh's court. Another famine would strike Canaan, and his brothers who had previously betrayed him ended up before him, literally begging for his help. Joseph not only forgave them, famously telling them, "What you meant for evil God has turned for good," but he also rescued his family and several other Jews by allowing them to escape the famine of Canaan by moving to the prosperous land of Egypt.

This marks the beginning of the Jews' return to Egypt. Through the years, their standing eventually changed, and the Jews would become slaves to the Egyptians. This, of course, leads us to the man we are told chronicled these ancient histories of the Israelites in the first place (whether you choose to believe the veracity of them or not)—the biblical patriarch Moses.

Chapter 1 – The Grand Exodus

"In a Jewish theological seminar there was an hours-long discussion about proofs of the existence of God. After some hours, one rabbi got up and said, 'God is so great, he does not even need to exist.'"

—Victor Frederick Weisskopf

As it pertains to what can be gleaned from the scriptures, the next major epoch in Jewish history refers to an unlikely patriarch named Moses. According to scripture, Moses had an unlikely beginning. The pharaoh of Egypt decided to reduce the burgeoning Jewish population in Egypt, and he planned to do this by ordering "every Hebrew boy that is born" to be thrown "into the Nile."

Three-month-old Moses was indeed placed in the Nile River, but he wasn't tossed in there to drown. His mother carefully put him in a basket and sent him floating on the waters. Moments later, the pharaoh's own daughter caught a glimpse of baby Moses floating in his basket. When she saw the child, her heart was stirred, and she felt compassion for him. Instead of letting the infant perish, she gathered up the basket and adopted Moses as her own.

In fact, she was the one who named him "Moshe" or "Moses," which was an Egyptian word for "son." In a similar fashion as to what had happened to the biblical Joseph, this reversal of fortune led to

Moses being raised in the pharaoh's court, with all the power and prestige that came with it.

However, upon reaching maturity, Moses began to investigate the hardships placed on his biological brethren. While surveying the enslaved Israelites hard at work, Moses bore witness to an Egyptian slave driver viciously assaulting a Jew. To see his own people abused in such a manner caused something to snap inside Moses, and without thinking, he killed the vicious Egyptian.

He tried to cover up the act by burying the slain Egyptian, hoping that nothing would come of his actions, but the next day when he returned to the worksite, where the Jewish slaves were already busily toiling for the Egyptians, it became clear that the word had already gotten out. The scripture tells us that this time around, Moses saw two Jews fighting each other, and after trying to break them up, one of them, irked by the interference, shouted, "Who made you ruler and judge over us? Are you thinking of killing me as you killed the Egyptian?"

Since Moses was now a known murderer, he fled to the town of Midian. Here, scripture tells us that the renegade Moses was taken in by a kind shepherd named Jethro. Moses gets along well with Jethro and his family—so much so that he marries Jethro's daughter, Zipporah, and has a child with her. It's unclear how long Moses stayed in his self-imposed exile in Midian, but the scripture states, "During that long period, the king of Egypt died. The Israelites groaned in their slavery and cried out, and their cry for help because of their slavery went up to God."

It was apparently after the king of Egypt had passed away that Moses had a close encounter with God. Moses was out in the wilderness tending Jethro's sheep when an object that the scripture describes as a "burning bush" appeared in the desert and began to speak to him. The voice emanating from the strange anomaly ordered Moses to go back to Egypt, inform the Hebrews that their liberty was at hand, and demand that the Egyptians set the Jews free.

Despite the awesome phenomenon before him, that of the eerily illuminated "burning bush," Moses was skeptical. Instead of simply accepting the word of God, he began to debate the supernatural force that had struck up a conversation with him. At one point, Moses asks the burning bush, "Suppose I go to the Israelites and say to them, 'The God of your fathers has sent me to you,' and they ask me, 'What is his name?' Then what shall I tell them?"

The answer to Moses's inquiry was stunning, and it would later become the centerpiece of much philosophical debate. For the voice from the burning bush responded, "I am what I am. This is what you are to say to the Israelites: 'I AM has sent me to you.'" The voice in the burning bush declared itself to be "The Great I AM." This would be important in later religious and metaphysical debates because it would serve as an answer to the very origin story of God himself.

Many cultures around the world have long struggled with the question of where their god (or gods) came from. Their religions, which no doubt utilize concepts with which they were already familiar, typically have stories in which a god was somehow birthed or created by another god. This, of course, creates an obvious conundrum since you constantly had to have one god before another. Otherwise, where did the god before them come from?

However, the God of the Jews solves this dilemma by having no beginning and no end. It's beyond human understanding how something like God can just exist, but even though mere mortals are not equipped to grasp it, the burning bush confirms to Moses that he has no backstory. When asked the question, "Where are you from? How did you get here?" God simply responds, "I am."

It's really no secret that existence is one of the greatest mysteries that humans struggle to solve. No science or religion has ever adequately explained how anything in our physical reality is even possible in the first place. If you believe in science and the Big Bang, we can trace the origins of the physical universe to a finite molecule that exploded and expanded into the universe some thirteen billion years ago, but no scientist can tell you where that molecule came from. Just like no theologian can tell you where God came from.

Thus, it's simply impossible for us to understand how *something* can come from *nothing*. Yet despite the seeming impossibility of it (and everything else's existence), the burning bush emphatically declares, "I AM." God is basically telling Moses, "I exist whether you understand it or not! I am!"

With these newfound revelations, Moses headed back to Egypt and consulted with the leaders of the Hebrews. Moses was meant to be the spokesperson for the Jews, but he complained of having "faltering lips." This is apparently a reference to a stuttering problem Moses had, which made public speaking difficult for him. For this reason, Moses requested someone to go with him to speak at the pharaoh's court. His own brother, Aaron, was chosen for this task. It must be remembered that even though Moses was adopted by the Egyptians, his long-lost brother Aaron had remained with Moses's biological family.

Moses and his brother Aaron went to the court and stood before the pharaoh. They imparted upon him the news that none other than the creator of Earth had given them divine instructions to tell the ruler of Egypt to let their people go.

As one might already know, the pharaoh had a "hard heart" and did not listen to these heartfelt pleas. According to scripture, this rejection provoked God's wrath, and Egypt was subjected to several plagues, including one in which a "death angel" passed by Egyptian homes and killed every firstborn Egyptian child. Meanwhile, Jewish families were instructed to put lamb's blood on the sides and tops of their doors so that the death angel would pass over them. Whether you choose to believe the veracity of the alleged event or not, it is an important moment for Jewish history, as this is the origin of the Jewish holiday of Passover. Since the death angel "passed over" their homes, the Jews were spared of God's wrath.

After these plagues devastated the region, the pharaoh, who lost his firstborn son during the final plague, had finally had enough, and he agreed to let Moses and his people go. They packed up their belongings and set out on their journey, which they hoped would lead to something better.

But right when Moses and all who followed him were in the desert, still beginning their journey to the Promised Land, the pharaoh suddenly changed his mind and sent his forces to intercept them. The scripture then describes one of the greatest miracles of the Bible: the "parting of the Red Sea." With the Red Sea in front of them and with Egyptian troops gathering behind, the Jews had nowhere to go. God, working through Moses, parted the Red Sea and allowed the Jews to walk across the dry sea bed.

Although it took a moment, the stunned pharaoh got over his shock at the sight before him and sent his army in pursuit. But as soon as the Jews crossed safely, the waters crashed back into place, killing the Egyptians who dared to follow.

Chapter 2 – Making Good on the Promised Land

"The soul, when accustomed to superfluous things, acquires a strong habit of desiring thing which are neither necessary for the preservation of the individual nor for that of the species. This desire is without a limit, whilst things which are necessary are few in number and restricted within certain limits; but what is superfluous is without end."

—Moses Maimonides

After leaving Egypt, scripture tells us that the Israelites marched through the Sinai Desert, but they were sidetracked in the desert wilderness for forty years. It was only after four decades had passed that the Jews reached the Promised Land of Canaan. Moses had died by this time and was replaced by a man named Joshua. Joshua led the Jews across the Jordan River and to the city of Jericho.

This was the site of a famed biblical story. In Jericho, the Jews marched around the city, clapping, shouting, and playing trumpets until the walls came tumbling down. The more skeptical among us, of course, would probably not pay too much heed to such accounts. However, regardless of one's beliefs, Jericho is indeed a real city. The remnants of the city can be found in Israel, and archaeologists have combed through the wreckage and have come to the conclusion that this human settlement dates back some 11,000 years.

If this is true, this means the city was already ancient when Joshua led the Israelites to its walls 3,000 years ago. For the Israelites, taking Jericho was the first step in taking over the entire land of Canaan. After they took the city, they then launched three major military campaigns that resulted in seizing power over the entire country. The first campaign was launched right after Jericho was taken, and it led to the seizure of all the surrounding land in central Canaan. The second campaign then went south to take out the nearest threats, while the third sealed off the northern country from potential attacks.

In light of the Israeli-Palestinian conflict of modern times, some Palestinians have pointed to what they claim to be an unlawful Jewish seizure of Canaan, which is directly documented in the scriptures, in an attempt to paint the Israelis as invaders and occupiers from the very beginning. Some Palestinians have even tried to claim that the Palestinian people are descended from the Canaanites. However, it's really not that simple. For one thing, the Jews had lived in the land of Canaan prior to their exodus from Egypt. Remember, Abraham had settled in Canaan long before Moses led the enslaved Jews out of Egyptian lands. In essence, they were returning to the land in which Abraham's covenant had been established. Furthermore, there were Jews who had never left Canaan in the first place, those who were already in the land when their previously enslaved brethren returned. So, while you can debate whether or not the Israelites were right or wrong in the wars they waged, to say that they were nothing more than invaders and interlopers is inaccurate. The history of the Jews is much more complicated than that.

At any rate, the first form of governance that the Jews established upon their arrival in Canaan was a confederation of twelve loosely connected tribes. The only central authority that existed for this confederation was their monotheistic belief in God, whom they called "Yahweh." The twelve tribes were connected by their faith in God and nothing more. They would routinely hold councils with each other to work out problems, but they were, for the most part, on their own, and they governed the different sections of Canaan separately.

However, over time (in this case around 1000 BCE), certain leaders called "judges" emerged, who were said to have "judged" Israel when such rulings were needed. These judges were actually local leaders who were given the power to adjudicate and make determinations when issues arose in the land. The most famous of these judges, who are mentioned in the Book of Judges in the Bible, were "Othniel, Shamgar, Deborah, Gideon, Tola, Jair, Jephthah, Ibzan, Abdon, Ehud, Elon, and Samson."

Of these judges, Western audiences are no doubt most familiar with Samson, who was known for being the great warrior seduced by Delilah. Although this judge's larger-than-life story seems almost too unreal to believe, some recently unearthed archaeological evidence, such as the so-called "seal of Samson," seems to support the claim that Samson did indeed exist.

This confederation of tribes stewarded over by judges lasted for several years before the last judge, the prophet Samuel, was commissioned by God to find a man who would be king of all the people of Israel. It was decided that Israel needed a king in order to fend off repeated attacks by the neighboring nations. In particular, a group of Semitic people called the Philistines had proved themselves to be a formidable enemy to the Israelites, as they repeatedly launched devastating raids on the Jewish territory.

In order to stand against the Philistines, it was believed that a central authority figure was needed to unite the tribes. Samuel chose a man by the name of Saul to fulfill this role. King Saul, the first king of Israel, would prove to be a conflicted and troubled man. Initially, he was quite good at doing battle with the Philistines, but it also appears that he was quite mentally imbalanced. Saul would often have episodes of depression, irrational anger, and a severe lack of judgment.

These things led the last living judge, Samuel, to regret his choice. Samuel then found a new potential leader for Israel in the form of a shepherd boy named David. The young man became a heroic fighter for Israel. In the scripture, David famously "slew the giant" named Goliath in a battle against the Philistines.

At first, Saul was happy to have David fighting for Israel, but it wasn't long before Saul became jealous of the warrior's growing popularity. This led to David being driven out of Saul's court. However, even though David was in exile, he was still just as popular as when he was a member of Saul's entourage. Soon, David managed to establish a large following of men who were willing to fight and die for their beloved leader. Saul attempted to use his army to hunt David down, but David's band of guerilla fighters continued to evade him.

In the meantime, Saul led a major battle against the Philistines, which ended in his defeat. Saul's sons were killed, and Saul himself was critically wounded after this battle, with the enemy closing in. Rather than be captured, Saul committed suicide. This led to David—who never ceased being popular with the common people of the land—becoming the king of the southern portion of Israel, known as Judea or Judah. He would soon get the consent of the northern tribes as well, effectively making him the king of all of Israel.

Since any proper kingdom needs a capital, David chose a centralized location in Judea for his, which he named the "city of peace." The Hebrew word for peace is "shalom." This would have made the name of his capital Jeru-Shalom, and one can see a similarity between this name and what the city would one day be called—Jerusalem. However, for easier readability, the city will be referred to as Jerusalem from this point onward.

As the king of a unified Israel, David proved himself to be a formidable king. Soon after he took the reins, all of the surrounding antagonists took note. The Philistines, Moabites, Ammonites, Edomites, and Amalekites all feared the might of King David.

Scholars have long thought that the Bible was the only source that mentioned King David. However, an artifact known as the Tel Dan Stele, which was discovered in 1993 in Damascus, Syria, dramatically changed that opinion. The Tel Dan Stele dates back to around 1000 BCE, and it is inscribed in Hebrew with the words "House of David." This seems to indicate that the biblical King David certainly existed.

David was eventually succeeded by his son, Solomon, who, around the year 966 BCE, built the first Jewish temple. The Jewish temple was meant to be the focal point of the Jewish religion. It was here that animal sacrifices were made to God, and the temple was also the center of religious life.

However, Solomon had many wives, and many of these wives came from foreign countries, where foreign religions reigned supreme. Pressured by his wives, Solomon began to build shrines and altars to foreign deities on the very grounds of the temple. This was viewed as an outrage by many. In addition, Solomon's grand construction projects in Jerusalem had caused severe taxation, which led to even more unrest. By the time Solomon was succeeded by his son, Rehoboam, Israel had broken into an open civil war, with the northern section of the country breaking away to wage war on the south. One of Solomon's own former court officials, a man named Jeroboam, led the charge and was made the ruler of the ten tribes of northern Israel, while Solomon's son Rehoboam, who ruled from Jerusalem, struggled to maintain what was left of his kingdom in the south.

The northern kingdom was actually known as "Israel," and it would keep this title until the two kingdoms eventually reunited. The northern kingdom would last for some 200 more years before being wiped out by the Assyrians around the year 721 BCE. The last ruler of the north was a monarch named Hoshea, who ruled from the northern capital of Samaria. During Hoshea's reign, Israel (again, we are referring to northern Israel) was essentially nothing more than a vassal state to the Assyrians.

When Hoshea attempted to defy the Assyrians and not pay tribute, the great Assyrian king Sargon II ordered their destruction. This brought the whole Assyrian army down on Hoshea's realm, utterly destroying the northern kingdom. The southern kingdom of Judea, in the meantime, would continue on, being ruled by a series of monarchs from the line of David, until around 587 BCE when the Babylonian conquest, followed by the Babylonian captivity, ended the monarchy.

In many ways, the defeat of the northern kingdom of Israel was much more devastating to the Jews than the capture of the southern kingdom. When the Assyrians stormed into northern Israel, they destroyed virtually everything in their wake, and they deported most of the population. The survivors were exiled, killed, or intermarried into oblivion until the ten tribes of northern Israel effectively ceased to exist—forever becoming known as the "ten lost tribes of Israel." This left just the two tribes in Judea. These two tribes were defeated by the Babylonians in 587 BCE, but although they were knocked down, they weren't knocked out. They would continue to eke out an existence in what would become known as the "Babylonian captivity."

Chapter 3 – From Babylon to the Abomination of Desolation

"There was Eleazar, one of the leading teachers of the law, a man of great age and distinguished bearing. He was being forced to open his mouth and eat pork, but preferring an honorable death to an unclean life, he spat it out and voluntarily submitted to the flogging, as indeed men should act who have the courage to refuse to eat forbidden food even for love of life. For old acquaintance' sake, the officials in charge of this sacrilegious feast had a word with Eleazar in private; they urged him to bring meat which he was permitted to eat and had himself prepared, and only pretend to be eating the sacrificial meat as the king had ordered. In that way he would escape death and take advantage of the clemency which their long-standing friendship merited. But Eleazar made an honorable decision, one worthy of his years and the authority of old age, worthy of the grey hairs he had attained to and wore with such distinction, worthy of his perfect conduct from childhood up, but above all, worthy of the holy and God-given law. So he answered at once: 'Send me quickly to my grave.'"

—2nd Maccabees 6: 18-24

The initial conquest of the Babylonians was absolutely devastating, as it resulted in a massive loss of life and the destruction of Solomon's Temple. But in the immediate aftermath, the Babylonians proved to be much more merciful conquerors than the Assyrians were. The Babylonians not only allowed Jewish culture to survive, but they also encouraged it to flourish. Instead of forgetting who they were, the Jews retained their full history. The Jews from former Judea were known as Judeans, and it was the term "Judean" that was eventually simplified to "Jew."

For about seventy years, the Jews lived and worked in the foreign land of Babylon, and many of them did quite well. They started their own businesses and engaged in commercial trade. Jewish scholars also became heavily involved in the intelligentsia, rendering service to Babylon's great libraries and even serving as members of the royal court. The culture of the Judeans did not disappear, as the Jewish communities in Babylon absolutely thrived.

But whether they wished for it or not, the Babylonian captivity would eventually come to an end. The ruler of Babylon was about to be surpassed by his own personal nemesis, the ruler of neighboring Persia: Cyrus the Great. King Cyrus sent his troops to take Babylon in 536 BCE, bringing an end to Babylonian hegemony in the region. But fortune still smiled upon the Judeans because Cyrus proved to be an even more benevolent ruler than the Babylonians had been.

Cyrus not only tolerated Jewish religion and culture; he also allowed the Jews to return to Judea. Once the Jewish people returned to Jerusalem, work to rebuild the ruined temple began almost immediately. The second temple would ultimately be finished in 515 BCE. This kicked off a period of religious refinement for the Jews in Jerusalem, in which their religious texts and practices were reaffirmed.

This period of Jewish reform under Persian hegemony came to a close around 334 BCE when a Macedonian Greek known as Alexander the Great sent his armies to conquer the holdings of the Persian Empire. Alexander was able to ultimately defeat Persian

Emperor Darius III, and from the wreckage of the deposed Persians, Alexander created his own sprawling empire, which stretched as far east as India and as far south as Egypt. Israel was no longer under the dominion of the Persians; it was now under the control of Alexander.

Alexander not only conquered nations but also founded great cities, the most famous of which bore his name: the Egyptian metropolis of Alexandria. The city of Alexandria would become an important one, not just for the Greeks but also for the Jews. Ever since the days of the Babylonian captivity, much of Jewish life had shifted from the agricultural sector to more of a merchant life, which was centered around big city ports. As such, for many, Alexandria became the perfect place to set up shop.

But the draw of Alexandria was not just for business. Alexandria had the Great Library, making the city a place of learning and drawing scores of Jewish thinkers to its great halls to perfect their philosophies. At the outset, Alexandria also espoused a fairly just society with toleration of different peoples and different modes of thought. Alexandria soon became one of the greatest focal points of Jewish life, second only to Jerusalem itself.

Alexander the Great's rule would prove to be brief, as he abruptly became ill and perished at the age of thirty-two. Before he passed, he had the presence of mind to divide his empire among his generals so that they could better rule the vastness of the land he had conquered. As it pertained to Israel, the inheritor of its control fell to General Ptolemy, who would control the lands of what today makes up Israel, as well as most of Syria, Phoenicia, and Egypt.

After Ptolemy came many generations of dynastic rulers, one of who was a dictator by the name of Antiochus Epiphanes. He came to rule over Israel around 175 BCE. By most accounts, Antiochus was a ruthless ruler, and his transgressions were captured most powerfully in the Jewish Books of the Maccabees.

Antiochus wished to "Hellenize" the Jews. In other words, he wanted them to more effectively assimilate into Greek culture. Most of the nations that conquered the Jews allowed for a gradual assimilation process. Antiochus, however, wanted an immediate one. This meant that he attempted to force the Jews to change their religious practices and habits. As documented in the Books of the Maccabees, Antiochus tried to encourage the Jews to engage in Greek Olympic-styled sports. As ridiculous as it sounds, he also tried to force Jews to eat pork.

There was a sizeable portion of so-called "Hellenized Jews"—in other words, Jews who readily adopted Greek culture—who argued with their countrymen over the merits of becoming more palatable to the Greeks. The First Book of Maccabees, which was written by a Judean faction who was dead-set against Hellenization, was, as you might imagine, not well disposed to this group.

In the First Book of Maccabees, a writer describes it as the following. "At that time there appeared in Israel a group of renegade Jews, who incited the people. 'Let us enter into a covenant with the Gentiles round about,' they said, 'because disaster upon disaster has overtaken us since we segregated ourselves from them.'" The writer of the First Book of Maccabees demonstrates the social dilemma facing the two sides of Jewish society during his day.

There were those who felt they should more readily conform to Greek society, while others, who were more conservative, wished to be a people set apart, a people who continued their traditions as before. Antiochus was well aware of this struggle, and he backed the more liberal Hellenized Jews, as he wished to drive the more conservative wing out of Judea entirely.

Antiochus eventually gathered up an army and marched on Jerusalem, storming into the very center of Jewish belief—the temple— in the year 169 BCE. He ruthlessly pillaged the temple of all of its valuables. According to the First Book of Maccabees, Antiochus carried off "the golden altar, the lampstand for the light, and all its utensils. He took also the table for the bread of the Presence, the cups for drink offerings, the bowls, the golden censers, the curtain, the crowns, and the gold decoration on the front of the temple; he stripped it all off. He took the silver and the gold, and the costly vessels; he took also the hidden treasures that he found. Taking them all, he went into his own land."

This brazen act understandably led to great unrest in Judea, and riots erupted against Greek rule. The forces of Antiochus then returned, and a great slaughter ensued. Antiochus's army installed a formidable walled citadel right in the middle of Jerusalem, where they could stand watch and directly exert their will upon the populace. According to the First Book of Maccabees, it was shortly after this that Antiochus issued a "decree" in which he made his intentions clear. "The king then issued a decree throughout his empire: his subjects were all to become one people and abandon their own laws and religion."

With this decree, Antiochus had launched an outright assault on Jewish identity. Some of the Hellenized Jews complied and essentially abandoned the old ways of their religion to embrace Greek culture and religious practices. This meant they no longer followed ancient Jewish practices, such as circumcision (a practice the Greeks utterly despised), and began to openly make sacrifices to Greek gods. To the shock of orthodox Jews, pagan altars were even set up in the Jewish temple.

This was obviously something that conservative Jews would not be able to tolerate. According to the First Book of Maccabees, Antiochus even appointed special "superintendents" that were in charge "over all the people" and who "instructed the towns of Judaea to offer sacrifice." This would then culminate in the infamous "abomination of desolation," which took place in the temple. To the horror of the orthodox Jews, a pig was actually slaughtered on the altar as a sacrifice to pagan gods right there in the Holy of Holies. This was indeed an "abomination" of "desolation" for those who witnessed it.

Some 160 years later, Jesus would later reference this event in what seems to be a warning of a potential recurrence in the future. In Mathew 24: 15-18, Jesus warns, "When ye therefore shall see the abomination of desolation, spoken of by Daniel the prophet, stand in the holy place. Then let them which be in Judea flee into the mountains."

The First Book of Maccabees then goes on to relate that despite the challenges the Jews faced, strong resistance against this abomination was formed. It was led by a Jewish priest named Mattathias Hasmon. Mattathias was just a common priest, but he would be thrust into the role of revolutionary leader when one of the "superintendents" sent by Antiochus attempted to force him to offer up a sacrifice to the Greek deity Zeus. Mattathias refused, but a more obliging Jew stepped forward and did as instructed.

Outraged, Mattathias struck down and killed both the "Hellenized Jew" and his Greek overseer. This event launched a rebellion against the Greeks, with Mattathias shouting to all who would listen to him, "Follow me! Every one of you who is zealous for the law and strives to maintain the covenant!" And they did. The scripture tells us that Mattathias and all who would follow him fled to the mountains, much as Jesus would later describe when he later referenced the event.

In their mountain stronghold, those who dared to defy the Greeks put up a resistance. The next major event to occur during this standoff was when Mattathias himself passed away in 166 BCE. Mattathias was then succeeded in leadership by his son Judas Maccabaeus, which roughly translated means "the Hammer." He was named such due to his fierce determination to shake off his foes. Judas was certainly ready to lay the hammer down on the Greeks for good.

Often described as a "military genius," Judas was able to take what seemed like certain defeat against a larger force and turn it into a victory. Judas Maccabaeus was ultimately able to retake Jerusalem. However, upon entering the temple, he and his men were appalled to see it "profaned" with pagan statues and burnt offerings. They immediately busied themselves with the task of cleansing the temple grounds and trying to set things right. While they were doing this, they sought to relight the candles of the menorah.

Initially, it seemed that there was only enough oil to light the lamp for one day, but somehow—almost as if by a miracle—the oil lasted for eight days. This feat would forever be commemorated in the Jewish holiday of Hannukah, which has one candle of the nine-branch menorah lit for each of these eight days, with the ninth spot being a helper candle that is used to light the other wicks. After freeing themselves from Greek dominion, the Jews then made an alliance with another new power: the Roman Republic.

Although the mighty empire that Rome would build had not yet come to fruition at this time, the Roman Republic was still a power to be reckoned with in its own right. And just as the Greeks began to weaken, the Romans became stronger. Thus, the Jews hoped to forge a friendship with the Romans in order to keep the Greeks and any other would-be enemies in check.

This treaty of friendship is clearly documented in the First Book of Maccabees. According to Maccabees, a representative of Judas named Eupolemus journeyed to Rome and spoke before the Roman Senate prior to the agreement being made. Eupolemus brought back a bronze tablet inscribed with the terms of the treaty. The treaty read as follows:

> Success to the Romans and the Jewish nation by sea and land forever! May sword and foe be far from them! But if war breaks out first against Rome or any of her allies throughout her dominion, then the Jewish nation shall support them wholeheartedly as occasion may require. To the enemies of Rome or of her allies the Jews shall neither give nor supply provisions, arms, money, or ships; so Rome has decided; and they shall observe their commitments, without compensation. Similarly, if war breaks out first against the Jewish nation, then the Romans shall give them hearty support as occasion may

require. To their enemies there shall be given neither provisions, arms, money, nor ships; so Rome has decided. These commitments shall be kept without breach of faith. These are the terms of agreement which the Romans have made with the Jewish people. But if, hereafter, both parties shall agree to add or rescind anything, then they shall do as they decide; any such addition or rescindment shall be valid.

The Jews entered into an agreement with the Romans thinking that they would gain a powerful ally who would help them stand against their enemies. But in good time, they would find that they had entered into a Faustian bargain. At first, the Jewish nation was little more than a protectorate of Rome, although it ultimately became a vassal state of the Roman Empire.

It is perhaps for this reason alone that the Books of the Maccabees were later excluded from the Hebrew Bible. As important as the story of Judas Maccabees, the "abomination of desolation," and the miracle of Hannukah might have been, the blatant pledge of undying loyalty to the Romans, as presented in the First Book of Maccabees, must have been too irksome for later compilers to include. In the ensuing years, Rome became the mortal enemy of the Jews, as the Romans destroyed their temple and kicked them out of their homeland. Thus, the Books of the Maccabees and its praise of the Romans might have been just too much to bear. It is most likely for this reason that the Maccabees were ultimately excluded from the Hebrew Bible. (There are eight Books of the Maccabees in total, but only the first two talk about the history of this period, with both of them offering similar yet slightly different accounts.)

The Hasmonaean dynasty, which was first established by Mattathias Hasmon, was ancient Israel's last gasp of independence. The Hasmonaean dynasty lasted for about eighty years before it was completely swallowed by their former ally of Rome. In 63 BCE, the Romans took advantage of the widespread corruption and infighting that had emerged in the Hasmonaean kingdom, which allowed them to put their thumb on the scales of Israel's history and take over the land for themselves.

Chapter 4 – The Beginnings of Roman Rule

"At times the truth shines so brilliantly that we perceive it as clear as day. Our nature and habit then draw a veil over our perception, and we return to a darkness almost as dense as before. We are like those who, though beholding frequent flashes of lightning, still find themselves in the thickest darkness of the night."

—Moses Maimonides

In the year 63 BCE, Roman General Gnaeus Pompeius Magnus, better known simply as Pompey, laid siege to the city of Jerusalem. At the time, Pompey was part of the famous Triumvirate, which was an alliance of three powerful men, which included himself, Roman General Marcus Licinius Crassus, and the famed Julius Caesar. Just a few years prior, in around 67 BCE, Israel's Hasmonaean Queen Alexandra had passed away. Her death marked the end of the last stable ruler of that dynasty, ushering in instability, and her prospective heirs struggled to maintain control.

In the meantime, the Roman legions had been pushing into nearby Syria on various military campaigns waged against Rome's enemies in the East. General Pompey had been tasked with putting down the threat posed by Tigranes II of Armenia and Mithridates VI of Pontus. Both of these nations would soon be rendered client states of Rome. After they were trounced, it wasn't long before Rome began to look toward Judea in the south. They knew it wouldn't take much to topple the Hasmonaean dynasty, as it was floundering.

After Queen Alexandra's demise, her son, John Hyrcanus II, became king, but any support he had among the citizens of Judea was rather weak. He was not a popular leader, so faith in him as a ruler was considerably low. He was also challenged by his younger brother, Aristobulus, who felt that the reins of power should be his. So much so, in fact, that he led an all-out rebellion against his brother, which culminated in a climactic battle outside the walls of Jericho.

When the forces of Hyrcanus began to waver, many of his own troops began to switch sides and join up with the forces of Aristobulus. Hyrcanus was ultimately forced to capitulate, and Aristobulus became the king in around 66 BCE. However, it wasn't long before Hyrcanus began plotting for his throne once again. He teamed up with one of his high-ranking court officials, a man known as Antipater the Idumaean (the same Antipater who fathered the famed King Herod), to find a way to knock Aristobulus from the throne.

In their efforts, they recruited the local ruler of the Arab region of Nabatene, Aretas III, to raise up an army against Aristobulus with Hyrcanus's pledge to restore territory that previous members of the Hasmonaean dynasty had taken. Aretas III, true to his word, raised up an army of some 50,000, which was then sent to march on Jerusalem. The first engagement was a decisive defeat of Aristobulus, who ended up having to seek refuge in the city while his foes circled the gates.

Just as all of this was going down, General Pompey was campaigning in nearby Syria. Hearing of these developments in Judea, he sent his general, Marcus Aemilius Scaurus, to see what was happening. Interestingly enough, as soon as Scaurus and his troops arrived onto the scene of this fratricidal civil war, emissaries from both would-be Jewish kings contacted him and implored the Romans for aid. Scaurus decided to put his thumb on the scale in favor of Aristobulus.

Various reasons for this decision have been offered. Romano-Jewish historian Titus Flavius Josephus later suggested that Scaurus was simply bribed and paid off by Aristobulus to do his bidding. But others have pointed out that it was probably just the most strategic thing for Scaurus to do since it would have been easier for him and his army to drive out the invading forces aligned with Hyrcanus than to launch a lengthy siege of Jerusalem. It is also likely that Scaurus felt this was the most politically sound move on his part since Aristobulus was currently seated as the monarch in Jerusalem. It would have been much more palatable for him to report back to General Pompey that he helped secure the current leader of Judea rather than having to admit to joining an uprising and overthrowing the incumbent king.

At any rate, due to the bitter civil war raging in Judea, the direct foreign intervention of the Romans commenced. Once Scaurus chose a side, the power of Rome was enough to convince Hyrcanus's and Aretas's armies to give up the fight, and they retreated to the Syrian city of Damascus. In Syria, John Hyrcanus II and his crew would come into contact with Pompey around 64 BCE.

Incredibly enough, Hyrcanus II was able to reverse his fortunes and gain a sympathetic ear from Pompey. In a tremendous reversal, General Pompey decided to side with Hyrcanus after all. Pompey's reasoning for siding with Hyrcanus is just as difficult to decipher as his subordinate Scaurus's initial decision to side with Aristobulus. But one factor that seems to have moved Pompey to turn against Aristobulus was the fact that there were reports that Aristobulus had been allowing piracy in the area. Since part of General Pompey's mission had been to stamp out piracy in the Mediterranean region, it might have made sense to get rid of one of the main sources of piracy: Aristobulus. At any rate, Pompey sent his troops to Jerusalem, and

Aristobulus, realizing he had just been beaten at his own game, attempted to surrender to the Romans. But although Aristobulus was ready to throw in the towel, his followers were not.

Outraged at the thought of Romans marching on Jerusalem, the supporters of Aristobulus slammed the gates shut and forced the Romans to lay siege to the city. The Romans, albeit with some effort, were able to break the siege, killing some 12,000 Jews in the process. Aristobulus was then taken captive, and Hyrcanus was installed in his place. But rather than giving Hyrcanus II back his power as king, the Romans made him the high priest of Jerusalem instead. This made him little more than a figurehead; in other words, the Romans were now effectively governing Judea.

To Pompey's credit, he refrained from looting the city, left the temple unmolested, and assured the priesthood that the Romans would not interfere with the Jewish religion. However, from this point forward, Judea was considered to be an extension of the Roman province of Syria, and as such, it was expected to pay an annual tribute to Rome.

In the meantime, the Jewish religion had become decidedly split between the more Hellenized Jews and the more conservative Jews. The liberal branch of Judaism was known as the Sadducees, and the more conservative, law-based wing was known as the Pharisees. This sharp ideological divide would only grow under the instability of Hyrcanus's rule.

Although they were fixed under Rome's wing, the Jews still, at times, played a vital role in the region. When the Triumvirate between Julius Caesar, Crassus, and Pompey broke down (Crassus died in 53 BCE, after which Pompey outright challenged Caesar), Hyrcanus sided with Caesar after he defeated Pompey. Hyrcanus's associate Antipater then ingratiated himself further with Caesar by sending him 3,000 foot soldiers during one of his campaigns in Alexandria.

Antipater the Idumean was duly rewarded by Caesar. He was given Roman citizenship and a special place in Caesar's heart. This distinction only grew when Caesar decided to make him the "first Roman Procurator of Judea." This made Antipater a high-ranking civil administrator akin to a governor, at least in the eyes of Rome. This good standing was also transmitted to Antipater's son Herod, as Herod was made the governor of the region of Galilee in 47 BCE. Julius Caesar would be assassinated a few years later in 44 BCE, and soon after, the Roman Republic would become the Roman Empire.

In 40 BCE, a new claimant to the throne would arise when Antigonus—the son of the deposed Aristobulus—sought to take back his father's throne. Antigonus was quite successful when it came to tapping into popular unrest over Roman taxation and into the manipulation of foreign intrigue. These were the two factors he used to connive his way to the throne of Judea.

The major enemy of the Romans at the time, the Parthians, sent Antigonus 500 some troops, which he used to remove Hyrcanus and install himself as the king. This led Herod to flee to Rome, where he gained the support of the Roman leader Mark Antony. Herod then returned to Judea in 39 BCE and waged war against Antigonus.

By 38 BCE, Galilee was back under Herod's control, and from there, he pushed on toward Jerusalem itself. With the help of the Romans, Herod took Jerusalem, and the deposed Antigonus was sent to Rome in chains, where he was eventually executed. Herod was installed as a Roman-friendly potentate who would become known as "Herod the Great." However, as you will soon find out, not everyone thought of him in that way.

Chapter 5 – A Jewish Man from Galilee

"God did everything necessary to get Herod's attention. He sent messengers from the East and a message from the Torah. He sent wonders from the sky and words from scripture. He sent the testimony of the heavens and the teaching of the prophets. But Herod refused to listen. He chose his puny dynasty over Christ. He died a miserable old man."

—Max Lucado

King Herod was, without a doubt, one of the most hated kings Israel ever had. He was viewed as a Roman puppet from the very beginning, and there were always internal plots simmering against him just below the surface. But regardless of how unpopular Herod may have been on the home front, in many ways, history records him as being a shrewd and practical leader who achieved quite a bit.

It was Herod, after all, who restored order to Israel, shored up the country's defenses, and invigorated the economy by establishing a robust trade market with Israel's neighbors. Herod also successfully walked the tightrope of keeping Rome happy while still making sure that the Jewish people had enough freedom to practice their way of life and religion inside their own homeland.

Herod is also credited with engaging in the important remodeling of the Jewish Temple, although these efforts were overshadowed in the minds of many because he decided to fly a Roman banner from the temple's gates, an incident that provoked a riot among the Jews, which Roman troops then had to subdue. Thus, Herod's legacy is at best mixed, but the worst attributes generally attributed to Herod are the claims of brutal despotism.

Herod was known for quickly putting down his perceived political enemies in Israel. And if the scripture of the New Testament of the Holy Bible is to be believed, he even went so far as to put them down before they even had the chance to grow up. After all, Herod plays a central role in the Nativity story that tells of the birth of Jesus Christ. According to scripture, Herod was visited by three "wise men" from the East—most likely Persians—who informed him that they had a vision that a new king had just been born.

During this time of oppression at the hands of the Romans, there had been much talk in Judea of the coming of a messianic king who could deliver them from their oppressors. The crafty Herod pretended to be thrilled with the news, but in reality, he seethed with jealousy and anger just below the surface. He was the king, and he did not want anyone else to rise up and depose him. However, for the sake of appearances, he pretended to be glad to hear of this alleged prophecy being fulfilled, although deep down, he was most certainly not too thrilled.

According to scripture, Herod then consulted with his "chief priests" and asked them, "Where is it that the Messiah is to be born?" The priests indicated that the prophets had foretold that a great leader would be born in Bethlehem. With this bit of prophetic intel, Herod then returned to the three wise men and informed them that the birth of the king they had envisioned would take place in Bethlehem. Herod instructed them, "Go and make a careful inquiry for the child.

When you have found him, report to me, so that I may go myself and pay him homage."

But although Herod pretended to want to pay the child king homage, in reality, he actually wanted to put an end to the child's life. The scripture then relates how the three wise men went to Bethlehem as planned. According to scripture, the means through which they located the home that housed baby Jesus was by following the "Star of Bethlehem." However, a casual read of the passage lets one know that this was not just any normal star, for this star moved across the nighttime skies and appeared to hover right over the home in which the baby slept.

The giant balls of nuclear fission floating in outer space—more commonly known as stars—are certainly not capable of entering into Earth's atmosphere and hovering over our homes. Our own sun is a medium-sized star, and it is 1,287,000 times larger than Earth. Like any other star, the sun is also really hot. Earth would be incinerated if it came anywhere near a star. Also, any star would be tremendously bigger than our own planet, which makes the idea of a star entering our atmosphere impossible.

This has led many modern skeptics to outright discount the story. However, just because it couldn't have really been a star in the astronomical sense, it still could have been some other form of extraordinary phenomena that the three wise men simply thought was a star. Some believe it could have been the conjunction of Jupiter and Saturn, a comet, or a supernova. One also has to keep in mind that the ancient chroniclers of these events were merely describing what they saw in terms that were understood during their time. Meteors, after all, have long been called "shooting stars," even though obviously today, we realize that they are not stars at all.

And for the sake of believers, if God was indeed behind this miraculous event, it could have been any number of miraculous phenomena that was used to lead the wise men that night. The account of the Star of Bethlehem, like much of the rest of scripture, is open to interpretation, and it's the reader's choice whether to believe it or not.

Having said that, according to the biblical account, the Star of Bethlehem led the three wise men to baby Jesus, and the three Magi bestowed all sorts of wonderful gifts upon the slumbering child. These three mystics from the East received yet another vision. In this one, they were instructed not to return to Herod and to secretly depart for their homeland without being seen. These instructions were apparently given in order to prevent Herod from finding out the exact location of the baby Jesus.

Scripture tells us that when Herod found out he had been duped by the Magi, he was pretty upset. He was furious that he had missed his chance to slaughter a future rival in their infancy, and he immediately ordered that all children "two years or less" be killed in the city of Bethlehem. Jesus's parents also received a vision and were warned of what Herod had planned. As a result, they were able to gather up baby Jesus and leave the city.

Shortly after Jesus was delivered to safety, King Herod died, therefore ending the threat that he posed. However, official historical sources list Herod's death as occurring around 1 BCE, although some believe he died in 4 BCE or even 5 BCE. This can be a bit confusing since our modern dating system was basically devised around Christ's birth—we have BC (Before Christ) and AD (Anno Domini, or "in the year of our Lord"). Many recent scholars prefer to use the terms BCE (Before Common Era) and CE (Common Era), but the fact remains that the original distinction was based upon the birth of Christ. Regardless of the terminology used, the fact remains that our historical calendar hinges on this one event.

So, having said that, it can be rather confusing to think that Herod might have died in 1 BCE, yet scripture says that he perished after Jesus was born. Yet even more confusing is the fact that many scholars insist that Jesus was born in the year 4 BCE! Christ was born *before Christ?* How does that happen? The truth is no one knows exactly when Jesus was born or when Herod died. The whole BC/AD system was created by a monk named Dionysius Exiguus in 525 CE. Dionysius himself did not know the exact date and simply used the best estimates he had on hand. For the time being, we will just have to let the archaeologists and scholars continue to debate this one out.

At any rate, after Herod's death, Roman Emperor Augustus allowed Herod's children to succeed him, thereby establishing the so-called Herodian dynasty. A beneficiary of this dynasty was Herod's son, a man named Herod Antipas, who was given control over the region of Galilee. This was, of course, the same Galilee in which Jesus was brought up.

Herod Antipas played a role in Christ's time on Earth. After Jesus was arrested in Jerusalem on the orders of the high priest, he was taken to the Roman procurator Pontius Pilate. The scripture tells us that Christ's accusers came before Pilate and complained, "His [Jesus] teaching is causing disaffection among the people all through Judea. It started from Galilee and has spread as far as this city."

At the mention of Galilee, Pilate's ears perked up. He knew that this meant Jesus was under the "jurisdiction" of Herod Antipas. Scripture tells us that Herod just happened to be in Jerusalem at that time, so Pilate decided to send Jesus over to be questioned by him.

According to the scripture, "When Herod saw Jesus, he was greatly pleased, because for a long time he had been wanting to see him. From what he had heard about him, he hoped to see him perform some miracle. He plied him with questions, but Jesus gave no answer. The chief priests and the teachers of the law were standing there, vehemently accusing him. Then Herod and his troops ridiculed and mocked him. Dressing him in an elegant robe, they sent him back to Pilate."

Herod Antipas was apparently fascinated by the stories he had heard of Jesus healing lepers, giving sight to the blind, and raising people from the dead. Herod, who apparently was not at all concerned about the accusations that the religious elite had leveled against Jesus, was just excited to be around someone who had such an extraordinary reputation.

But as Jesus stood silent before him and refused to indulge his curiosity, the mystique wore off. Herod's initial interest gave way to open mockery and ridicule. He put a royal robe around Jesus's shoulders to taunt those who called Jesus a king and sent him back to Pilate. Pilate, now aware that, despite his mischief, Herod had found no real reason to condemn Christ, insisted that he did not want to condemn him either.

Nevertheless, the religious authority of Judea was outraged and demanded that action be taken. As the scripture tells us, it was this conflagration of events that resulted in Jesus being led to the cross. Now again, since the Bible is the only real document we have of many of these things, one has to decide whether to follow the account that follows. However, regardless of what one believes when it comes to the Bible, the majority of modern scholars believe that Jesus did, in fact, exist, and many Abrahamic religions, especially Islam, treat Jesus as an important figure in their beliefs.

Christians believe that Jesus rose from the dead on the third day after he was crucified. He appeared to his disciples, talked, laughed, and even ate with them, before giving his final sermon and ascending to heaven. The Acts of the Apostles, also known as the Book of Acts, states that "he was lifted up, and a cloud took him out of their sight." This is where the biblical narrative of Jesus, a Jewish man from Galilee, ends. And it was from his extraordinary life that a brand-new sect of Judaism, which would become known as Christianity, truly began.

Chapter 6 – The Emergence of Christianity from Judaism

"Every man should view himself as equally balanced: half good and half evil. Likewise, he should see the entire world as half good and half evil. With a single good deed, he will tip the scales for himself, and for the entire world, to the side of good."

—Moses Maimonides

This book is about Jewish history. But it must not be forgotten that Christian history *is* Jewish history. After all, Jesus was Jewish, his disciples were Jewish, and most of his early followers were Jewish. To omit the story of how Christianity sprung from the Jewish religion would be a travesty to Jewish history itself. Christianity was initially just a small religious movement known by those in mainstream Judaism as the "Nazarene sect" due to the fact that Jesus hailed from the city of Nazareth in Israel's region of Galilee.

After Christ left the scene, the early Christians were initially led by one of Christ's original disciples, a man named Simon Bar-Jonah, whom the rest of the world probably knows better as Peter. Peter's birth name was Simon, and his father's name was Jonah. The word "Bar" is the Hebrew term for "son." Thus, the name "Simon Bar-

Jonah" translates as simply "Simon, son of Jonah." It was Jesus who gave Simon Bar-Jonah the name of Peter. Jesus actually called Peter "Cephas," which is an Aramaic word that means "rock." Since the Christian New Testament first appeared in the Greek language, translators replaced "Cephas" with the Greek word "Petros." In later translations, the name would become Peter.

The Bible tells us that this nickname came about on an occasion in which Jesus and his disciples discussed what the people were saying about Christ's ministry and what his purpose really was. The disciples chatted amongst themselves about how some were saying that Jesus was the return of John the Baptist, Elijah, Jeremiah, or some other powerful prophet. Jesus then asked his followers an open question, "Who do you think I am?" Simon Bar-Jonah spoke up and declared, "You are the Messiah, the son of the living God." Jesus was pleased with Simon's words and told him that, for now, he would be "Cephas" or "Petros," depending on the translation, the rock on which he would build his church.

Here are the verses from the scripture in which this all plays out:

> When Jesus came into the coasts of Caesarea Philippi, he asked his disciples, saying, "Whom do men say that I the son of man am?" And they said, "Some say that thou art John the Baptist: some, Elijah; and others, Jeremiah, or one of the prophets." He [Jesus] saith unto them, "But whom say ye that I am?" And Simon Peter answered and said, "Thou art the Christ, the son of the living God." And Jesus answered and said unto him, "Blessed art thou, Simon Bar-Jonah! For flesh and blood hath not revealed it unto thee, but my father which is in heaven. And I say also unto thee, that thou art Peter [the rock], and upon this rock I will build my church; and the gates of hell shall not prevail against it."

—Mathew 16:13-19

The scripture that names Peter as the "rock" on which the church would be built is very important for the Catholic Church in particular since they would come to view the Apostle Peter as none other than the first pope. The merits of such a notion are, of course, highly debatable, but it stems from the fact that Peter was said to have traveled to Rome and established a church just prior to being arrested by the Romans and executed.

If this story is true, another irony is the historical narrative that St. Peter's Basilica was literally built on top of Peter's bones, thereby fulfilling the prophecy of Jesus's words, "upon this rock I will build my church." As recently as 2019, the Vatican has affirmed its belief that they are indeed in possession of St. Peter's final remains. But again, these things are still open for debate.

As it pertains to scripture, the biblical narrative tells us that although Jesus had conferred such great things upon Peter, he ended up failing miserably on multiple occasions. This is in no way a means to disparage Peter; it is merely an accepted—and even celebrated— biblical truth. One of the reasons people tend to love and identify with Peter so much is because of his human frailty and failures.

The scripture tells us that although Jesus charged him to lead the church, soon after Jesus was arrested, a very frightened and alarmed Peter tried to distance himself from Jesus and famously denied knowing him. In fact, Peter claimed ignorance of even knowing who Christ was when questioned about it three separate times. After Christ was crucified, Peter hid in fear and despaired, thinking that all was lost. The scripture then describes how the resurrected Jesus appeared before Peter and the rest of the disciples, and Peter's doubts, fear, and anguish turned to faith and rejoicing.

In one of the last alleged encounters Peter had with Jesus, Christ held him to account for his previous denial. Jesus asked Peter three times, "Do you love me?" These probing inquiries into his dedication was a direct response to Peter having previously denied Christ three times. Each time Jesus asked, Peter would respond, "Yes, I love you."

Jesus asked again, and Peter assured him, "Yes, Lord, you know that I love you." Jesus asked a third time, and Peter even more emphatically stated, "Lord, you know all things; you know that I love you." At which Jesus then commissioned Peter to steward the faithful, telling him, "Feed my sheep."

Jesus revealed to Peter what some believe was a direct prophecy of what he would have to face at the end of his ministry. Christ told Peter, "I tell you the truth, when you were younger you dressed yourself and went where you wanted; but when you are old you will stretch out your hands, and someone else will dress you and lead you where you do not want to go." Again, although it has never been proven, it was said that Peter was executed by the Romans by being crucified upside down. Such a death would indeed have Peter with his "hands stretched out."

The biblical Acts of the Apostles documents what happens next in Peter's early ministry. Rather than being meek and mild, a bold and confident Peter began to preach right in the temple. Rather than denying Christ out of fear of being arrested, Peter loudly proclaimed his name for all to hear. Eventually, Peter was arrested and sent to answer to High Priest Caiaphas as to what he was up to. Peter didn't back down and once again proudly proclaimed the message of Christ. He could have been stoned on the spot, but Peter was a changed man, and nothing anyone did or said could deter him from preaching the gospel.

Scripture tells us that although the priests in the temple did not believe in Peter's message, they were greatly impressed with his "eloquence." They knew that Peter, a fisherman by trade, "was not an educated man." They were stunned that someone like him had become such a powerful speaker. For the moment, the temple authorities decided to let Peter off with a warning. They told him that they would let him go, but they insisted that he stop proselytizing to the masses about Christ.

As one might expect, Peter wasn't going to listen, and as soon as he was turned loose, he was boldly preaching the teachings of Christ all throughout Jerusalem. Peter was later arrested again, and the scripture tells us that this time, he was spared by a Pharisee named Gamaliel. Gamaliel is an important figure in Jewish history, and he is mentioned in several sources outside of the Bible, as his wisdom was celebrated by many. And on this encounter with Peter, it was apparently on full display. In regard to what should happen to Peter and his fellow disciples, Gamaliel cautioned his peers.

> Men of Israel, take care what you are about to do to these men. For before these days Theudas rose up, claiming to be somebody, and a number of men, about four hundred, joined him. He was killed, and all who followed him were dispersed and came to nothing. After him Judas the Galilean rose up in the days of the census and drew away some of the people after him. He too perished, and all who followed him were scattered. So, in the present case I tell you, keep away from these men and let them alone, for if this plan or this undertaking is of man, it will fail; but if it is of God you will not be able to overthrow them. You might even be found opposing God!

Quite cleverly, the great mind of Gamaliel had reasoned that if Peter and his company were just blowing a bunch of smoke, it would all evaporate of its own accord. If, on the other hand, they were divinely inspired by God, there wouldn't be anything they could do to stop this divine commission even if they wanted to. Due to Gamaliel's solid logic, Peter and his companions were set free once again.

As fate would have it, Gamaliel would play an important role in another great Christian apostle: the Apostle Paul. Paul, whose birth name was "Saul of Tarsus," was quite an interesting figure in Jewish history. In many ways, Paul always seemed destined to stride two worlds. Although he was a strong believer in the Jewish faith, being born in the heavily Hellenized city of Tarsus meant he was also a

Roman citizen. He spoke Greek and was well aware of Greco-Roman culture and values.

Before becoming a Christian, Paul was a budding Pharisee under the tutelage of that other great Pharisee, Gamaliel. It is said that Paul began his training under Gamaliel as a young man, shortly after his bar mitzvah. Although his own teacher famously preached restraint when it came to sanctioning the new Christian sect, Paul, before his conversion, was one of the most zealous persecutors of the faith.

Rather than show restraint, Paul literally hunted Christians down. He had them thrown in prison, beaten, and even stoned to death. It's for this reason that his "road to Damascus" conversion was such a dramatic reversal. According to scripture, Paul was on his way to Damascus to break up and arrest Christian congregations when he allegedly had a vision of Christ. Christ asked him, "Saul? Saul, why are you persecuting me?" Paul initially had no idea who the apparition was and asked, "Who are you, Lord?" To which the brightly illuminated figure responded, "I am Jesus who you are persecuting."

This visionary experience supposedly led Saul to change his name to Paul and become a Christian. And he didn't just become a Christian—he became the greatest Christian missionary the world would ever know. Paul ended up traveling all over the Roman Empire, preaching the gospel to all who would hear it. Whether he was speaking in Hebrew or Greek, he was openly proclaiming the teachings of Christ.

It was largely the efforts of Paul that helped Christianize the non-Jewish populations of the Roman Empire. This segment would only grow over time, and soon, non-Jewish Christians would outnumber Jewish Christians. By the 4th century CE, when a Roman emperor named Constantine came to the throne, Christianity would not only be accepted but become the official religion of the empire.

The transformation of this obscure religious sect from Judea into the official religion of one of the most powerful empires was just about as dramatic as Paul's conversion. Gamaliel had openly wondered if Christianity was just a fad that would come to nothing, but once Christianity emerged from Judaism, it most certainly proved itself to be far more powerful of a force than most imagined it would.

Chapter 7 – Destruction and Diaspora

"Be careful in your relations with the government; for they draw no man close to themselves except for their own interests. They appear as friends when it is to their advantage, but they do not stand by a man in his time of stress."

—Gamaliel

There was a major seat change that took place in Judea in 64 CE with the establishment of a new Roman procurator of Judea: Gessius Florus. Roman procurators were viewed by the general populace as foreign interlopers and were generally disliked, but Gessius Florus proved to be even more despised than was usually the case. His administration was thoroughly corrupt, and dissent in Judea was commonplace under his leadership. One of the most adamant Jewish dissidents during this period was a group called the Essenes.

The Essenes believed that an apocalyptic war between the forces of good and the forces of evil was about to take place, and they were preparing for the final showdown. Rome, sensing the trouble that was brewing, sent Cestius Gallus, the governor of Syria, who essentially held the keys to Rome's eastern frontiers, with a large and capable

Roman legion force to take on any threats in the region. Cestius Gallus arrived in Jerusalem just in time for Passover in 65 CE.

For the Jews of this period, the Passover festival was a time in which the city was not only packed with observant Jews for the holiday but also rabble-rousers and revolutionaries who threatened to set off the powder keg of discontent that Judea had become. About as soon as Gallus arrived, he was met with crowds of demonstrators, who shouted out their grievances against Gessius Florus.

It's important to note how important this outspokenness of the Judeans during this period really was. In previous times, many would have been afraid to speak out, but so many people had reached their limit with the Roman administration that much of the reservation from previous years was gone. The Romans, who were always on guard for invasions from external enemies on their frontiers, did not wish to have to quell local disturbances if they did not have to. So, to some extent, the Romans were tolerant of demonstrations against their governance. The situation was a standoff at best.

As it pertained to his visit, Gallus wished to make sure that the procurator Gessius Florus was not unduly antagonizing the local population. As part of his fact-finding mission, he met with local Jewish leaders so that he could speak with them directly about what life was like under Florus. Gallus heard them out and pledged to ensure that Florus behaved himself in a just manner. However, this was basically lip service, as Gallus turned around and left without implementing any changes.

As one can imagine, these superficial efforts to keep the peace didn't amount to much, and the Roman fears of revolt would come to fruition in 66 CE. When the despised Roman administrator of Judea, Gessius Florus, faced several episodes of protesters, instead of giving in to any of their demands, he cracked down on them, and he cracked down hard. In an effort to humiliate the Jewish people, he demanded to be given a tribute from the funds of the Jewish Temple. There did not seem to be any reason for this sort of request, making this outright extortion.

In the meantime, word of the unrest once again reached the ears of Cestius Gallus, the governor of Syria. He sent some of his representatives back to Judea to assess the situation. They found that large demonstrations were taking place in which Jews were demanding independence, as well as an "embassy to Rome" in which they could state their grievances against Florus directly.

The Jewish protesters were indeed getting bold by this point, and it seemed like the whole thing could blow up at any second. After one particularly brutal crackdown, the conflagration finally erupted. The streets were filled with Jewish protesters, who, due to their large numbers, managed to push out the occupying Roman soldiers. A group of Jewish revolutionaries known as the Zealots then stormed a Roman garrison and took control of the strategic fortress of Masada.

Here, they were able to solidify their position and take advantage of a massive stockpile of weapons. The absolute point of no return then occurred when a zealot by the name of Eleazar ben Simon ordered all of the Roman hostages that were being held to be killed in cold blood. The revolutionaries now knew that the full force of Rome would come down on them, and they prepared themselves for the inevitable siege. As a result of these events, Gallus, the governor of Syria, was once again dispatched to Jerusalem. This time, it was not to keep the peace but rather to wage an all-out war against the rebels.

However, the Zealot forces were able to outsmart Gallus and launched a successful ambush of his troops as they approached their stronghold. Gallus's army was crushed. This was an incredible victory for the Jews, but Roman Emperor Nero wasn't going to give up simply because a few legions were destroyed. Instead, he cobbled together more troops, this time under the command of his top general, Vespasian, and sent them on a crash course with the Zealots.

Vespasian's first battle occurred in Galilee in 67 CE, where he encountered an army of some 50,000 Jews led by a priest named Josephus. The army was defeated, and Josephus was taken hostage. Josephus would later become a Roman historian and write down much of the details of these events. After laying waste to Galilee, Vespasian stormed down the Israeli coast and subdued cities such as Joppa and Jericho before heading east to Jerusalem.

General Vespasian was stopped in his tracks when he received word that Emperor Nero was dead. Nero had actually taken his own life. Due to the uncertain situation in Rome, Vespasian halted his advance and returned to the Roman capital. In the meantime, his son, Titus, was left in charge of the Roman forces in Judea. Vespasian would ultimately become the emperor himself, after which he then ordered Titus to march on Jerusalem, a campaign that commenced in 70 CE.

Titus had an army of some 80,000 Roman soldiers surround the city, and with some effort, they eventually smashed through the city walls. This led to a prolonged siege of the Jewish fighters who were holed up in the citadel, setting the stage for one of the most dramatic standoffs in history. Titus finally led the legions to victory that summer, taking over the city and burning the Jewish Temple to the ground.

As for the zealots holed up in the fortress of Masada? Right as the Romans came pouring in, they made the fateful decision to end their own lives. They killed their wives and children before committing suicide themselves. Sadly, they had come to the cold conclusion that they were better off dead than falling into the hands of the vengeful Romans. This was a devasting blow for the Jewish revolutionaries, to be sure, but the fighting spirit was not out of them yet. They still had one more massive uprising up their sleeve in the form of a charismatic man who was descended from David, whom they called the messiah— a man named Simon bar Kokhba.

This next major uprising, which took place in 131 CE, would become known as the Bar Kokhba revolt. Similar to the previous revolt, the Jews initially had successes in battle, but massive Roman reinforcements soon crushed the rebellion, and Bar Kokhba himself was killed. And the further repercussions for the Jewish people were absolutely devastating.

The Romans actually outlawed the practice of Judaism and kicked the Jews out of Jerusalem. Wishing to wipe all memory of Judea from the map, the Romans had the audacity to rename the region *Syria Palaestina* ("Palestinian Syria"), apparently as an insult to the Jews since it was a Roman variation of the Jews ancestral adversary—the Philistines. It was in the wake of this bitter apocalypse, which rocked their homeland to its very core, that the Jewish diaspora began in earnest.

Chapter 8 – The Talmudic Teaching of the Exiles

"There's a lovely Hasidic story of a rabbi who always told his people that if they studied the Torah, it would put scripture on their hearts. One of them asked, 'Why on our hearts, and not in them?' The rabbi answered, "Only God can put scripture inside. But reading sacred text can put it on your heart, and then when your hearts break, the holy words will fall inside."

–Anne Lamott

With the Jews scattered to the winds, the conquering Romans became hellbent on removing every last vestige of Jewish memory from the region. First of all, they named the territory *Syria Palaestina*. This was done as a form of mockery against the Jews since it was known that their ancestral foes had been the Philistines. Jerusalem was also renamed. Instead of calling it Jeru-Shalom—named the "city of peace" by King David—Emperor Hadrian renamed it Aelia Capitolina.

The word "Aelia" stems from Hadrian's family name of Aelius. Hadrian had a new Roman settlement built upon Jerusalem's ruins and then stamped his own family seal upon it. And it would remain

Aelia Capitolina until the Christian Emperor Constantine changed the name back to Jerusalem in the 4th century. Interestingly enough, future Muslim conquerors apparently didn't get this memo, for when the city was first claimed by the Muslims, it was often referred to as "Aelia."

No matter what anyone called their former capital, the Jewish people were learning how to live away from the land that had been the center of their faith and identity for several centuries. During this period, one of the greatest safe havens for the Jews proved to be Babylon. The very same land that they had been held captive during their famed Babylonian captivity became their greatest refuge when persecuted by the Romans.

Comprising much of modern-day Iraq, Babylonia, which was technically part of the Parthian Empire at this time, was still a bulwark of the East, protecting the Eastern lands against invasions by the Romans. Babylonian cities, such as Nisibis, Nehardea, Pumbedita, Sura, and Mahoza, all received a massive influx of Jewish immigrants during this period. The Jews of Babylonia even had their own chief community leader, who was known as the "Prince of Captivity" or sometimes called the "Exilarch." This man was in charge of community laws, religious activities, and even the collection of taxes among community members.

They also pooled together resources for the writing of a great religious work that would become known as the Babylonian Talmud. The word "Talmud" is a Hebrew term meaning "to teach." The Talmud was created at a time when the Jews were struggling to reorient their religion away from the physical location of Jerusalem and the ruined temple and into an ideology that they could package and take with them no matter where they may go.

One of the principal architects and facilitators of this new teaching was a man named Abba Arika, who founded a sprawling academic center in the Babylonian town of Sura, which boasted some 1,200 pupils. This institution would become the main center for Jewish learning in Babylonia. One of his most brilliant pupils was a man named Mar Samuel.

Mar Samuel was the child of an affluent merchant, and he himself grew up to become a prominent physician. He rejected the prevailing theory that "bodily humors" caused illness and instead attributed maladies to the presence of "minuscule particles that entered the human body through the air," making him a man ahead of his time. It was also the great mind of Mar Samuel that came up with some of the most vital diaspora laws, which dictated how Jews should conduct themselves while in exile.

The first diaspora law was known as the "Law of the Land." This law taught that Jews should faithfully adhere to the laws of the host nation that they found themselves in, as long as these laws do not force them to violate their religious beliefs. The second diaspora law then dictated that Jews shouldn't hesitate to defend their host nation, even if it caused them to come into conflict with another Jew from another nation.

This meant, for example, that if a Jew somewhere in the Roman Empire was drafted as a Roman soldier and then fought Jewish troops drafted into the Parthian army, neither one should have qualms with fighting the other since they were just doing the bidding of their host nation. The Talmud itself consists of two main parts: the Mishna and Gemara. The Mishna is the compilation of a long tradition of oral commentary on the Hebrew Bible, or Torah.

The oral commentary of rabbis seeks to explain parts of the Torah that might have been unclear. Bible verses that say things such as rendering out punishment for transgressions with an "eye for an eye and a tooth for a tooth" were clarified. Instead of taking such things literally, rabbinical commentary suggested that such expressions were metaphors for the need for equal justice, but they did not necessarily mean that someone would literally have to have their eyes put out in pursuit of it.

In addition to the Mishna, the Gemara is the documentation of further rabbinical discussion of the written rabbinical commentary. As one can see, the Talmud itself is quite a comprehensive analysis of Jewish learning. One of the most controversial aspects of the Talmud is its references to a figure called "Yeshu," which is an Aramaic variation of "Yeshua." Yeshua, of course, is the Hebrew name of "Jesus."

Some believe the mention to have been a depiction of Christ, and the references made in the Talmud are not exactly flattering. However, later Jewish scholars would refute this, insisting that the text was actually talking about a different "Yeshua" and not the one of the Christian faith. At any rate, this compilation and merger of the Mishna and Gemara would continue until the Talmud was considered complete in around the year 500.

The rest of the world had changed considerably in the meantime. The Roman Empire, which had initially persecuted both Jews and Christians alike, had adopted Christianity as its official religion. Ever since Roman Emperor Constantine issued the Edict of Milan in 313 CE, which accepted Christianity as a tolerated religion protected by Roman law, the empire became increasingly Christian in its makeup.

As such, there was a renewed interest in the land that Jesus himself had walked. Soon, Christians were pouring into the Holy Land to retrace those very footsteps. Holy relics were uncovered, and new Christian churches, such as the Church of the Holy Sepulchre, were erected to mark locations sacred to the faith. For the next few centuries, Christianity would reign supreme in Israel, while the Jewish people were mostly left on the sidelines.

However, the Roman Empire was growing weaker, and many regions were slipping from its imperial grasp. Soon, the capital of the Roman Empire was no longer Rome but rather a city in Asia Minor (modern-day Turkey) called Constantinople. This city, which was named after Constantine the Great, would be the seat of power for the Roman Empire's successor: the Byzantine Empire.

The Byzantine Empire was actually the Eastern half of the original Roman Empire, which was centered around the old Greek colony of Byzantium, of which Constantinople was a part. But when the Western half of the Roman Empire fell to roving bands of Germanic tribes from western and northern Europe, technically all that remained intact was the Eastern half. Even though Rome fell in 476, the Byzantine Empire would last until 1453.

The powerful Byzantine Emperor Justinian I managed to reclaim much of the old empire during his reign in the mid-500s, but by the early 600s, a threat from the East would rise up to threaten Christian hegemony over the Holy Land. The Persian Empire, which had long been an enemy of the Romans, was on the march. And after several horrific clashes between the two empires, the Persians managed to march on Jerusalem itself, seizing control in 614 CE.

Byzantine Emperor Heraclius managed to launch a massive counteroffensive and retook Israel for Christendom in 630. The Byzantines, suspecting that the few Jewish residents who remained had collaborated with the Persians, redoubled their persecution against them. But little did anyone know that an unforeseen religious and political powerhouse was about to rise up from Arabia and change everything.

Chapter 9 – The Jews and the Rise of Islam

"When Allah will say: Oh Jesus, son of Mary! Remember my favor on you and your mother, when I strengthened you with the holy Spirit, you spoke to the people in the cradle and when of old age, and when I taught you the Book and the wisdom and the Taurat [Torah] and the Injeel [Gospel]; and when you determined out of clay a thing like the form of a bird by my permission, then you breathed into it and it became a bird by my permission, and you healed the blind and the leprous by my permission; and when you brought forth the dead by my permission; and when I withheld the children of Israel from you when you came to them with clear arguments, but those who disbelieved among them said: This is nothing but clear enchantment."

—The Quran/Surah V: 110 (The Food)

Anyone who has ever read the Quran will realize just how similar the stories and characters are to those in Judaism and Christianity. They are similar because they are basically summaries with slight alterations of the same people and events. The Quran speaks of Abraham, Noah, Moses, and Jesus in rapid-fire summaries interspersed with supposed divine commentary from God or, as the monotheistic deity is called in the Quran, "Allah."

This divine inspiration was supposedly transmitted through Allah's "final prophet," Muhammad. But who was Muhammad? Where did he come from? Muhammad hailed from a tribe of Bedouins in Saudi Arabia. Prior to the rise of Islam, Saudi Arabia was the home of a vast melting pot of religious beliefs. Most Arabs were polytheists who worshiped many gods. But even so, they were in constant contact with both Christians and Jews. After the destruction of the Jewish Temple and after many generations of the diaspora, several Jewish communities sprouted up in Arabia.

Muhammad was in contact with these communities, and he became a great admirer of the Jewish faith. Of course, Jews and Arabs have a long history of living together in the region, and both groups maintain the ancestral narrative that Abraham was the common father for both people groups, with Abraham's son Jacob going on to found Israel, while Abraham's other son, Ishmael, founded the Arab world.

Once the Jewish population increased in Saudi Arabia, the Jews became quite prominent in settlements on the Arabian Peninsula, such as Medina, which became a focal point for Jewish life and culture in the region. It also just so happens that Medina was the place from which Muhammad first developed the Muslim faith.

Muhammad was an orphan who was raised by his uncle. He grew up to be a shepherd before getting a job as a camel driver for an affluent widow by the name of Khadija, whom Muhammad ended up marrying. While driving camel for Khadija's caravans, Muhammad first encountered both the Jewish people and the Jewish faith. It was from them that he learned of the biblical stories of the Old Testament patriarchs, such as Abraham, Noah, Moses, and the like.

Besides the Jews, Muhammad also encountered members of the Gnostic Christian sect and learned variations of their accounts of the life of Jesus. This connection with Gnostic Christianity can, in fact, be quite easily proven because the Quran relates stories of Jesus that the Gnostic Christians promoted. The Quran, for example, tells the account of Jesus making clay bird sculptures and then bringing them to life as a child. If you are a mainstream Christian and have never heard the story of a young Jesus breathing life into clay birds, there's a reason for that—it's not a part of the mainstream Christian canon. This account is from the Gnostic Christian texts, which were excluded from what would become the official Christian Bible. Muhammad frequently encountered and discussed religion with the Gnostics during his travels, so this was how the Gnostic account of Jesus breathing life into clay birds made its way into the Quran.

At any rate, these strains of Judaism and Christianity found their way into the Quran to produce Islam, a monotheistic faith that believes in one God and a series of prophets, which include all of the sages of the Old Testament, as well as Jesus and the last and final prophet, Muhammad himself.

Muhammad was able to gain a growing following among the local Arab population, but to his chagrin, the Jews, upon whom much of his theology had been derived, were mostly not interested. To them, Muhammad's teaching, which largely recycled certain aspects of Judaism and Christianity, was just not appealing. Meanwhile, Muhammad ran into trouble in the city of Mecca when he began to preach against the idol worship that was going on in the city.

It is important to note the history of Mecca and just how strong polytheistic idol worship was in that city. Mecca, of course, would eventually become a holy city to Muslims. It is known for having the shrine of the Kaaba, to which millions of Muslims make a pilgrimage, known as the hajj, every year. The Kaaba, which is a "cube-shaped" stone structure, predates Islam. Islamic tradition contends that the Kaaba was built by none other than the Jewish patriarch Abraham and his son—from whom Arabs are said to have descended—Ishmael.

However, during Muhammad's day, the Kaaba actually housed stone idols that the polytheists worshiped. Muhammad was steadfastly against the use of the Kaaba for such purposes. This led to conflict with the city authorities, and Muhammad was forced to flee to Medina in 622 CE. Here, he and his followers attempted to get the local Jews to join the cause of Islam. But the locals refused, and Muhammad ended up unleashing his forces on them instead. Muhammad's disciples attacked the Jews and confiscated their goods and armaments. After solidifying his control of Medina, Muhammad then unleashed an assault on Mecca in 630 CE. His relentless struggle against Mecca proved successful, and soon, the polytheists at the Kaaba were put out of business. During his lifetime, Muhammad's teachings would reach the whole of the Arabian Peninsula.

Muhammad's faith could be aggressive, and it was not against forcing conversion by way of the sword. In fact, many Jews found themselves having to flee from the very faith that Judaism helped to inspire, as zealous Muslims attempted to convert them by force. It should be noted that Islamic law actually prohibits forced conversion, yet it still happened in history. Many believe that Muslims were more interested in conquest than conversion, but this is still an ongoing debate, and only time will tell as to what extent Muslims went to in order to gain new converts. Nevertheless, Islam spread rapidly, and by the time of Muhammad's death, his successors continued to carry the banner of Islam into neighboring countries.

The Muslim forces ultimately pushed into Israel—the former homeland of the Jews—and successfully wrested it from the Roman Byzantines in 637 CE. Muhammad was already dead by this time, but his dream of reaching all the way to the Holy Land had been achieved by his successors. With Muslim control of Israel secured, the ban that the Romans had placed upon the Jewish people was lifted, and many were able to return.

Muhammad's Muslim successors practiced a form of tolerance over the beliefs of both Christians and Jews. Immediately before the Byzantines pulled out of the area, the victorious Muslim general, Omar ibn al-Khattab, actually pledged his tolerance with an official declaration that read, "From Omar ibn al-Khattab—to the inhabitants of Aelia [Jerusalem]. They shall be protected and secured both in their lives and fortunes, and their churches shall neither be pulled down nor made use of by any but themselves."

Such words certainly make the Muslims sound like benevolent conquerors, but even though non-Muslims were tolerated, they were still treated as second-class citizens. Under Islamic law, Christians and Jews who refused to convert to Islam had to pay a special tax, known as the jizya, and were made to adhere to specific restrictions that the Muslim citizens did not.

Even so, for many Jews, just being allowed back in Jerusalem was worth having to pay a tax and being subjected to arbitrary rules and regulations. But even if second-class citizenship was deemed to be tolerable, the later generations of Muslim rulers soon tightened the screws on Jewish residents. The Jewish faced increasing levels of discrimination, leading many to leave the Holy Land for environs that were more hospitable.

It was actually when the Arab Muslims were displaced by Turkish Muslims from the East, in 1065, that the situation for both the Christians and Jews changed dramatically. The Turks were nowhere near as tolerant as the Arabs were, and soon, Christians and Jews were being subjected to outright attacks for their faith. Probably one of the most famous abuses of these Turks was when they began attacking unarmed Christian pilgrims who had come to the Holy Land to visit religious sites.

Ever since the initial conquest by Arab Muslims in 637 CE, Christian pilgrims were allowed to visit the Holy Land and were guaranteed protection by Muslim authorities. However, once the Turks took over, everything changed. Unarmed Christian visitors were being attacked, robbed, and kidnapped. These repeated outrages served as part of the pretext for Pope Urban II to launch the First Crusade.

The Byzantines, who had been fending off incursions by Turkish Muslims for some time, had already been asking Western Christians for aid, and so this, coupled with the harassment of Christian pilgrims, was enough to launch one of the bloodiest series of wars in history. And the consequences would be grave for the Jews just as much as it was for the Muslims.

Chapter 10 – The Crusades, Kabbala, and Maimonides

"Christians, hasten to help your brothers in the East, for they are being attacked. Arm for the rescue of Jerusalem under your captain Christ. Wear his cross as your badge. If you are killed your sins will be pardoned."

—Pope Urban II

Pope Urban II called for the First Crusade in 1095. The culmination of this call to arms was due to Muslim depredations against Eastern Byzantines and Christian pilgrims, coupled with the Catholic Church's long-held desire to retake the Holy Land for Christendom. This call to action struck a chord with Christian Europe, and all who heard it were immediately filled with an excited sense of being part of a great mission.

At this point in time, western Europe, which had been torn asunder after the fall of the Western half of the Roman Empire, was just now pulling itself up from the rubble. The barbarian tribes that had previously attacked imperial Rome had since become Christians, making Christianity the glue that held together not an empire but several loosely connected kingdoms. The major authority that the kings and queens of Europe looked to was not a Roman emperor but rather the pope of the Roman Catholic Church.

Countless European nobles answered the call to arms and promised Pope Urban II that they would build up armies as soon as possible to march for the Holy Land. However, professional armies take time to form, and they would not be able to set off all at once, but not everyone was willing to wait. Outside of what would become the main Crusader forces of Europe, those of the knights and kings, the common peasant class was galvanized by the message as well. Impassioned preachers, such as the notorious Peter the Hermit, were able to rouse the average person to stop what they were doing and head out on a "divine mission" to retake Jerusalem.

Peter's silver tongue convinced thousands to drop their farm implements, put down their baked goods, and follow him. Peter ended up having one of the most bizarre armies in history, as regular men, women, and even children followed him. Some of them were armed with nothing more than sticks, but all of them were absolutely convinced that they were going to drive the Muslims out of the land of Christ.

However, Peter's crusade is not officially counted as part of the First Crusade, which consisted of professionally trained troops sent to the Holy Land. Peter's ragtag group is a sideshow to the main event, and it has been referred to as the People's Crusade. Peter led his undisciplined mass of humanity through the countryside of Europe in the spring of 1096, where they caused general distress to all they encountered. With no way to feed this unruly bunch, order broke down, and many of them often stole from the locals.

Jews, in particular, were vulnerable to this mob since local authorities often failed or even refused to protect them. Of course, the Jews were also targeted because of their religious beliefs, and they were subjected to attempts of forcible conversion by the Christians. This was a time when anyone who practiced a different faith was viewed quite literally as the enemy, so it didn't take much for the

Christians to attack the Jews. And the heightened drama of the Crusades stirred up these sentiments more than ever before.

The first attacks on Jews by these makeshift Crusaders occurred in France and then continued into the Rhineland of Germany. It was here that some of the worst atrocities against the Jews were carried out. It has been estimated that over 12,000 Jews were killed in indiscriminate attacks launched by the People's Crusade. It must be stressed that the actions of this ragtag group of peasant crusaders were their own. They were thoroughly condemned by the pope, even though it was his call for a crusade that spurred them to act.

Nevertheless, by the time this group of would-be crusaders reached the Holy Land, the Turks made short work of them, killing or enslaving almost all of Peter the Hermit's band of misfits. Perhaps the only real benefit this debacle had for the larger First Crusade was that it caused the Turks to greatly underestimate the well-equipped professional Crusaders that would come after Peter the Hermit's miscreants bit the dust.

After the annihilation of Peter the Hermit's peasants, the first main Crusader force arrived on the scene. This group aggressively fought their way through Asia Minor and on into the Holy Land until they were right at the gates of Jerusalem itself. These Christian knights in shining armor were like nothing the Muslim warriors had encountered before. Muslim bowmen fired volley after volley of arrows at the approaching Crusaders, yet knights, whose metallic armor bristled like the coat of a porcupine, kept on coming.

The defenders of Jerusalem were forced to surrender, after which one of the worst Crusader atrocities against the Jews was committed. It is said that many of the Jews who remained in the city were herded into a synagogue. Then the Crusaders lit the building ablaze, killing all who were inside. The Crusaders would go on to maintain a presence in the Holy Land for approximately 200 years before they were driven out by Muslim forces.

Various Muslim rulers would then control the region until the Muslim Turks of the Ottoman Empire made Israel/Palestine a part of their dominion. It would remain so until the Turks were defeated in World War One, after which the British took control of Israel/Palestine in 1918. It would take another world war and a declaration by the United Nations to finally grant independence to a new Jewish state in 1948. But as it pertains to the Crusades and their immediate aftermath, the Jewish people had to go to great lengths just to survive.

In stark contrast to the Jews' turmoil in the Holy Land, the Sephardic Jews of Spain were doing quite well. The term "Sephardic" comes from the word "Sefarad," which is the Hebrew word for "Spain." Sephardic Jews had already been in Spain for centuries, prior to its Muslim takeover in 711 CE. But the years immediately before the Muslim Moors poured into the Iberian Peninsula from North Africa were not generally good ones for the Jewish people, as previously tolerant Christian rulers had tightened the screws on their Jewish subjects and had begun to persecute them. But once the Muslims took over, rather than persecution, the Muslim conquerors restored much of the freedoms the Jews had once enjoyed. To be clear, non-Muslims were still treated by their Muslim overlords as second-class citizens. Although they were second in every way to Muslim believers, Jews and Christians were allowed to practice their own faith and live according to their cultural beliefs unhindered as long as they paid a tax and recognized their subordinate status.

Today, such blatant discrimination would be abhorrent, but the second-class citizenry imposed by the Muslim rulers of Spain was actually much preferable to the outright intolerance of the many Christian rulers who came before, as they sought to forcibly convert Jews and directly interfere with their way of life. For many Jews, having to pay the Muslims a tax that essentially amounted to an extortionary protection racket was still the lesser of two evils and was considered preferable to the alternative.

At any rate, even as second-class citizens under Muslim dominion in Spain, over the next few centuries, Spanish Jews began to flourish. Since they were able to openly practice their religion and refine their intellectual pursuits, the Jews made great strides in medicine, science, philosophy, literature, and the like. The Jews also became known for providing skilled translators who provided linguistic links between Hebrew, Greek, Arabic, and Spanish texts as needed. They also spoke their very own version of Spanish, which came to be known as "Ladino." In fact, it was due to their efforts that many great ancient works, which had once been thought lost to the Dark Ages, were brought back into the light. Jewish commercial traders and bankers began to rise to prominence as well, and Spain began to boast prosperous and powerful Jewish communities. During this period, the Jewish intelligentsia also greatly expanded, and one prominent physician and academic, a man by the name of Hasdai ibn Shaprut, founded a Hebrew academy in the Spanish city of Córdoba. Hasdai was a great light that shined in the diaspora until his death in around 970.

At this time, Spain was under the control of the Umayyad dynasty, whose leadership was fairly benevolent and enlightened for their day. However, the Umayyad rule came to an end around the year 1031 and fractured off into various Muslim strongmen controlling their various corners of Spain. Nevertheless, the Spanish diaspora carried on, and in 1138, the greatest mind of the Sephardic Jews—Moses Maimonides—was born in Córdoba, Spain.

But although Moses was a Sephardim and was born in Spain, he did not spend most of his life on the Iberian Peninsula. When he was just a young man, the fierce fundamentalist regime of the Almohads took hold in southern Spain. The Almohads abolished the status of *dhimmi*, or the acceptance of second-class citizenship for non-Muslims, and instead gave Jews just three options: convert to Islam, leave the country, or be killed.

Even if a Jew converted to Islam, the hostile atmosphere created by the Almohads led to continued persecution and discrimination of Jewish converts. The Almohads even made Jewish converts don special, distinctive clothing so that they could be easily identified as Jews, which, of course, only opened them up to more ridicule by the Muslims. Such things are shockingly similar to how the Nazis of the 20th century forced Jews to wear the Star of David so that they could be easily identified in a crowd. It is indeed alarming at how frequently history repeats itself.

At any rate, this Muslim persecution led Moses to flee to the more hospitable environs of North Africa instead. He and his family initially settled in Fez, Morocco, before moving farther east. He eventually ended up settling in Egypt in 1166. At this time, Egypt was controlled by the Muslim Fatimid Caliphate, which proved to be much more welcoming than the Spanish fundamentalists.

Here, Moses soon established himself as a community leader in the Jewish diaspora in Egypt. It was here that he would produce great literary works, including his famed Mishnah commentary. The Mishnah, if you will recall, is a part of the rabbinical text known as the Talmud. More central to his current situation, Maimonides also expounded upon the debate over whether or not it was ethical for Jews to convert to Islam under oppression but secretly remain Jews. Many Jews in Spain could not leave the country, so they had been forced to do just that. When given the choice of conversion or death, they chose life and professed allegiance to Islam, yet they still secretly practiced their Jewish faith. The argument among the diaspora was whether or not such a practice could be condoned under Jewish law. Maimonides argued that it could, for in such a situation, one's choices were rather limited. Maimonides also argued that accepting a forced conversion was often the best choice for a Jewish family as a whole, as they could continue—at least in secret—to raise their children in the Jewish faith. If they had been executed for refusing to conform, their children might have been taken away from their surviving family members and forced to become Muslims. Not everyone agreed with Maimonides, with some claiming that the Talmudic scriptures were clear that Jews should "be killed rather than transgress."

Such matters remained a fiery debate for much of Maimonides's life. Some suspect that one of the reasons why it was so near and dear to his heart was that perhaps his family had actually made a false conversion to Islam before they were able to escape. There is no proof that this occurred, but it is certainly a possibility, and it would explain why such things mattered so much to Maimonides. If one had found that Maimonides had become a *converso* to Islam, he would have lost respect in the diaspora community, which often called for full resistance no matter the cost.

Besides his philosophical work, Maimonides would also become rather renowned for his treatises on medicine. During his time, he composed complex analyses of previously unknown diseases, such as diabetes, hepatitis, and asthma. Maimonides was a man who believed in rational scientists and looked toward Greek philosophers and physicians, such as Aristotle, as much as he did toward the patriarchs of the Bible.

He sought to create a more rational form of Judaism that used reason and logic as much as mysticism. But despite all of these efforts, a rival movement that was very much the antithesis of Maimonides's logic gained prominence in the diaspora community. This group was known as Kabbala. Adherents of Kabbala (also spelled as Kabbalah) sought a more mystical framework with which to see the world. Although the movement sprouted up in Maimonides's day, Kabbalists claim that their beliefs are derived from oral lore that dates all the way back to Moses and the Exodus. Needless to say, Moses Maimonides didn't agree.

Nevertheless, Kabbala gained prominence. And the most inspired writing related to Kabbala was that of the Zohar. This mystical, kabbalistic book first emerged in that great, medieval hub of Jewish learning—Spain. The Zohar surfaced in the 13th century, and it was compiled by a Jewish scholar by the name of Moses de León. However, it should be emphasized that Moses de León claimed not to be the author but rather just the compiler. According to Moses, he had managed to put together the much older work of a certain Rabbi Shimon bar Yochai, who dates back to 70 CE, around the time the Jewish Temple was destroyed by the Romans. It has been said that Rabbi Shimon bar Yochai hid in a cave for several years, where he received the divine inspiration to write the Zohar.

Like the Talmud, the Zohar is essentially another commentary, but rather than focusing on Jewish law, it focuses on Jewish mysticism. The Zohar takes a look at the supposed hidden meanings of scripture and offers up a mystical interpretation. Moses de León claimed that he had recovered this lost treasure and simply wanted to reveal it to the world. However, ever since this revelation has been made, many Jews, then and since, have been skeptical about the true origins of the text, with some openly wondering if Moses de León hadn't simply written it himself.

But no matter where it may have come from, the writings of the Zohar provide a rather unique interpretation of the scripture, one that is quite different than any other analysis hitherto provided. In the Zohar, every line of the Torah is scrutinized for a deeper, mystical/spiritual meaning. Just the first words of Genesis, "Bereishit bara Elohim..." (Hebrew for "In the beginning, God created...") launches us into the following, rather astonishing commentary narrative:

> At the very beginning the King made engravings in the supernal purity. A spark of blackness emerged in the sealed within the sealed, from the mystery of the Ayn Sof, a mist within matter, implanted in a ring, no white, no black, no red, no yellow, no color at all. When he measured with the standard of measure, he made colors to provide light. Within the spark, in the innermost part, emerged a source, from which the colors are painted below; it is sealed among the

sealed things of the mystery of Ayn Sof. It penetrated, yet did not penetrate its air. It was not known at all until, from the pressure of its penetration, a single point shone, sealed, supernal. Beyond this point nothing is known, so it is called "resishit" [beginning]: the first word of all...

The Zohar takes the first sentence of Genesis and produces a mind-boggling commentary of how all matter in the universe was created. For some, this sounded like divine inspiration, while for others, absolute madness. The interesting thing about all of this is that some of the language almost seems to match modern-day descriptions used by physicists when attempting to describe the Big Bang.

Just think about it. According to the Zohar, in the beginning, there was nothing until one spark of light exploded all of physical reality into existence. Physicists describing the Big Bang are basically describing the exact same thing. Physicists contend that the entire universe burst forth from one finite point, which was incredibly dense (dense enough to hold the mass of the entire universe) and under immense pressure. Notice how the Zohar mentions the "pressure of its penetration." For Kabbalists, that mystical finite point from which the universe sprung is the "Ayn Sof, a mist within matter."

Some other discussions in the Zohar also seem to describe what we term black holes and other cosmological discoveries that wouldn't take shape in the scientific world until just recently. The Zohar refers to these black holes in the cosmos as being "portals" into other domains. Although it has not been proven, some physicists would concur since they theorize that black holes could actually be passageways to parallel universes.

Whether you believe it or not, it is fascinating how anyone could come up with such things several centuries before science offered up theories that sound strikingly similar. Then again, maybe the writers of the Zohar just got lucky, and after throwing everything to the metaphysical wall that they could, some of it just happened to stick.

At any rate, by the end of the 12th century, due to the dominance of Kabbalistic circles in places such as France and Spain, many Jewish intellectuals who followed the more rational disposition of Moses Maimonides found themselves leaving Jewish scholarly circles altogether. This was especially the case in Europe, where droves left more traditional Jewish institutions in favor of continuing their pursuit of philosophy and scientific thought at Catholic-run institutions instead.

For you see, in this topsy-turvy world of shifting ideologies, it was now the Christians who were more tolerant of the Jews than the Muslims. The Sephardim once again began to excel in the fields of medicine, finance, and commercial trade. But this very success, especially those successes in the financial sector, led many average Spaniards to resent the Jews, as they saw the Jews as foreign interlopers taking resources away from them. These animosities, in addition to other issues, would come to a fever pitch by the time of the Spanish Inquisition.

Chapter 11: The Spanish Inquisition

"The numerous evils to which individual persons are exposed are due to the defects existing in the persons themselves. We complain and seek relief from our own faults; we suffer from the evils which we, by our own free will, inflict on ourselves and ascribe to God, who is far from being connected with them!"

—Moses Maimonides

Jewish life in Spain had gone through quite a metamorphosis in 500 years' time. At the start of the 11th century, they were living in a so-called "Golden Age" under benevolent Muslim rulers who accepted their unique culture and faith. Unfortunately, these Muslim overlords were superseded by much more narrow-minded practitioners of Islam, and by the end of the 12th century, the Jews were forced to flee for their lives if they wished to remain both alive and practitioners of the Jewish faith at the same time.

Many fled to North Africa, just like the great Jewish thinker Moses Maimonides, but others found their way to northern Spain, where the last bastion of Christian independence on the Iberian Peninsula remained. Initially, the Christians of northern Spain were tolerant of the Jews and even welcomed their expertise in fields such as medicine and finance. However, the Catholic grip on Spain began to increase, and by the 13th century, the so-called Reconquista—a crusade to take Spain back from Muslim conquerors—was in full swing.

The previously powerful Muslim strongholds of Córdoba and Seville were reclaimed by the resurgent Christians, leaving only the Muslim Emirate of Granada in southern Spain. Granada would finally be defeated in 1492, thereby officially ending the Muslim presence in Spain. In the meantime, as Christian dominance was reestablished, an inquisition into non-Christian elements that lurked below the surface began to take shape.

The Spanish Inquisition, a "Roman Catholic tribunal," was initially established to sift out "heretics" lurking among the Jews and Muslims who had recently undergone conversion to the Catholic faith. Those suspected of committing heresy by reverting back to their old faith were subject to scrutiny by the inquisitors. The accused were interrogated, sometimes tortured, and often left in dungeons until they confessed to that which they had been accused. It was a no-win situation for an accused converso. If they confessed, they would be condemned as a heretic, but if they did not confess, they would either be killed or languish in prison.

Conversos of all levels and stations were affected by this inquiry into the true nature of their faith. Even the famed Saint Teresa of Ávila, who hailed from a Jewish converso family, was questioned at one time by the Spanish Inquisition. And while the Jews faced intense persecution, mainline Spanish Christians suffered as well since the Inquisition created a paranoid atmosphere of suspicion and distrust. If anyone made a wrong move, their actions could be misinterpreted and reported to religious authorities.

Toward the end of the Inquisition, no one was safe from its paranoid grasp. It was probably the Russian author Fyodor Dostoevsky who captured the insanity of the Inquisition best in his poem, "The Grand Inquisitor," in which Jesus himself returns to

Earth—to Seville, Spain, in fact—only to face severe questioning from the Christian clergy.

Things eventually got so bad that the pope himself tried to intervene and limit the scope of the investigations into heresy. The abuses dished out by the inquisitors led to a massive refugee crisis among the Sephardic Jews of Spain, with many of them once again fleeing for their lives. Many ended up going as far east as Turkey, where it is said that the Ottoman Turkish Sultan Bayezid II welcomed the Jews wholeheartedly, as he was thrilled at the prospect of all of these highly educated "physicians, architects, businessmen, financiers, inventors, mechanics, and craftsmen" that he was receiving. It is said that Bayezid mocked the king of Spain, proclaiming, "Ferdinand has made his county poor and made ours rich!"

It really did prove to be a great boon for the sultan because just as Europeans were perfecting the first gun-based armies, Jewish engineers who had been kicked out of Spain arrived in Turkey to help impart this knowledge to the Turks. Interestingly enough, it was just as the Inquisition was heating up in 1492 that Spain embarked upon what would become the greatest achievement of the age when they commissioned a little-known sailor by the name of Christopher Columbus to find a new route to India.

A few decades prior, in 1453, the Byzantine Empire had been defeated by the Ottoman Turks, who seized the great city of Constantinople, eventually transforming it into their own capital, which they renamed Istanbul. But even more pressing for the rest of the world was that this meant the land routes that traditionally went through Byzantium were now blocked off by the hostile Muslim Turks who controlled Constantinople. This effectively cut off the ancient land routes that formed the Silk Road, which led to India and China.

As a result, the European powers were forced to find alternate routes to India. One plan was to sail all the way around the tip of southern Africa, but the waters were not safe due to the pirates who stalked the seas. Columbus proposed going straight west from the coast of Spain and sailing until he reached the other side of the known world—in other words, until he reached India. Columbus, like most educated individuals of the time, knew the world was round, although the flat-earth theory was still popular, especially among the lower classes. Columbus knew that he wouldn't sail off the edge of the planet; instead, he believed that if he kept going west, he would eventually end up in the East, thereby gaining access to India. Little did Columbus know that the earth was rather large and that there were a couple of continents in between his route to the East. Not to mention a whole multitude of people that Columbus would mistakenly call "Indians" (he really did think he was in India).

Columbus is a controversial figure today, considering the fact that he did not always treat the native inhabitants he encountered with the dignity they deserved. But one thing that is interesting about Columbus was that his true dream was to raise enough money for a new crusade to retake Israel. Columbus was indeed a passionate Christian, but some contend that Christopher Columbus was also a converso. Historians have struggled to figure out the exact details of his life, and his background has still remained rather mysterious. Some believe that Columbus hid his background on purpose because of the negative connotations that came with being a converso. This is all just conjecture at this point, of course, and hopefully, one day, more light can be shined on Columbus's past. However, there is one interesting fact that is often overlooked. Columbus's trip was heavily funded by two prominent Spanish conversos, Luis de Santángel and Gabriel Sánchez. They are said to have loaned some 17,000 ducats for the mission.

Christopher Columbus's crew also boasted many conversos, including his famed interrupter Luis de Torres. In fact, Torres has the distinction of being the first of the crew to step foot on American ground. After Columbus and his company spotted land, Torres was sent to the shore to scope out the terrain. At one point, he supposedly saw a strange, big bird walking around in the distance. As the story goes, Luis de Torres pointed at the bird and exclaimed the Hebrew word for "big bird," shouting, "Tukki! Tukki" If this account can be believed, it was due to Louis de Torres's apparent confusion that the American turkey got its name!

Whatever the case may be, the fate of the Jews who remained in Europe was rather bleak during this period. After being expelled from Spain, many traveled eastward, as mentioned earlier, some as far east as Turkey, which was under the dominion of the Ottomans. However, many more stopped short of Ottoman borders and settled in eastern Europe.

Poland especially became an enclave of Jewish habitation. Much of the immigration coincided with the reign of King Sigismund I of Poland, who proved to be a great benefactor of the Jews. His son, Sigismund II, who succeeded him in 1548, largely continued this benign treatment and even allowed some level of autonomy in the Jewish community in Poland.

However, here, we once again see a tragic cycle repeat itself. It started with local authorities tolerating—even welcoming—Jewish refugees, desiring the skillsets they might bring. But then, after a few decades, the Jews were once again marginalized and despised for their faith. Over time, as they continued to be increasingly oppressed in Poland, they were made to live in separate sections of Polish towns, which were called ghettoes. Jewish members of the diaspora could only hope and wait for their day of emancipation to arrive.

Chapter 12: Jewish Emancipation

"Both state and church have as their object actions as well as convictions, the former insofar as they are based on the relations between man and nature, the latter insofar as they are based on the relations between nature and God."

—Moses Mendelssohn

Ever since their expulsion from Jerusalem and the dawning of the diaspora, Jewish philosophers looked toward the day that they might experience full emancipation—the normalization of Jewish life within a non-Jewish-dominated society. It was around the time of the European Enlightenment that Jewish intellectuals were having an enlightenment of their own, which came to be known as the Haskalah (meaning "wisdom" movement), in which the topic of emancipation was furiously debated anew.

Intellectuals vigorously discussed how they could gain equal rights and called those who would listen to them to "come out of the ghetto." Those Jewish philosophers who stood against the discrimination and stereotypes lobbed against them argued that much of these criticisms came about as a result of the manner in which they were forced to live. They argued that if they could come out of the ghetto and simply live a normal life that the relations between Jews and non-Jews would immediately improve. Some European nations listened to the arguments being made, and Britain, in particular, made some progress in 1740 when Parliament passed a law that allowed Jews to be naturalized as citizens in British colonies. This was then followed up by a 1753 law that gave Jews the "right of naturalization" in Britain itself. Unfortunately, due to the massive public protest from Britain's non-Jewish population, this law was rescinded the following year, in 1754.

Right around this time, in 1729, one of the greatest—and perhaps unlikeliest—of Jewish emancipators emerged from a ghetto in the German town of Dessau. His name was Moses Mendelssohn. While growing up in the ghetto, Mendelssohn cut his philosophical teeth on the works of the Jewish intellectual giant Moses Maimonides, as well as an Enlightened titan from England, John Locke. Interestingly enough, Mendelssohn actually taught himself Latin just to read John Locke. Learning about Locke's thoughts opened up a whole new world to this child of the ghetto, and he was soon bound for Berlin, where he studied philosophy in earnest with the best of the Enlightenment thinkers.

During the course of his studies, Mendelssohn began to understand that the confines of the ghetto were limiting Jewish potential and that immediate emancipation was in order. He steadfastly believed that one of the keys of this emancipation was to get Jews to become fluent in the European languages of their host countries, such as the predominant language where he himself lived—German. In order to aid his brethren in these efforts, he went about the monumental task of translating the Torah into German. Also, realizing that many of the Jews in the ghetto did not know German letters, Mendelssohn went about "transliterating German words with Hebrew letters."

His transliterated German/Hebrew Bible caught on like wildfire. As soon as the younger generations in the ghetto grasped German, they began to then apply themselves to the Latin alphabet. Reading and writing in European scripts was finally unlocked for them.

Along with his efforts in teaching Jews European languages and letters, Mendelssohn also proved to be a great religious reformer, as he advocated for a kind of separation of Church and state. He was among the first to champion the idea that the Jews should separate rabbinical teachings from mainstream education. He also argued that "the breaking of a religious law" should be viewed as an "individual offense" and "not a state offense."

Many within the Jewish community embraced the ideas of Mendelssohn, but his more orthodox brethren viewed his teachings as treacherous and corrupting of the faith. He was lambasted as a "Jewish Faust striking a bargain with the devil—willing to eat the fruits of Western civilization at the price of losing his Jewish soul." His German translation of the Torah was not much appreciated either. The acclaimed Rabbi Ezekiel Landau of Prague denounced it outright as a "danger to Judaism." Nevertheless, Mendelssohn's ideas of both the Enlightenment and reform appealed to the younger generations and laid the groundwork for the larger reformation that would take place later on within Judaism.

While Mendelssohn sparked renewed debate in the German-speaking Jewish world, France, in the meantime, was in the midst of its own reformation, a reformation of the old order that would soon lead to outright revolution. There were an estimated 50,000 Jews in France at the time, and many of them were of Sephardic origin, having been expelled from Spain in the purge of 1492. At the dawning of the French Revolution, these Jews were given full citizenship—essentially full emancipation—for the first time. But the French Revolution proved to be incredibly unstable. After the French king literally lost his head, several others also lost theirs in quick succession as the terror of the French guillotine took hold. Out of this chaos eventually emerged a French general turned emperor: the famous Napoleon Bonaparte.

Many Jews worried that they would lose their newfound freedoms under Bonaparte, but as it turns out, as despotic as Napoleon may have been in other aspects of his reign, he was an enthusiastic supporter of Jewish emancipation. He demonstrated this sentiment shortly after taking power by requesting "an Assembly of Jewish Notables" to meet with him in order to discuss what their future in his empire might hold. During the discussion, the role of the rabbis in the ghettos was brought up, with Jewish leaders being asked if they had any special "police powers" over the populace and if their authority was derived from "Jewish law" or simply a habit derived from "custom." The Jewish assembly stated that the power the rabbis habitually wielded over the denizens of Jewish ghettos was not sanctioned by Jewish law but merely a custom that had developed over time.

Such an admission would play a pivotal role in emancipation since it marked the beginning of rabbinical authority shifting from outright control of the Jewish public to simply being spiritual guides. According to famed Jewish scholar Max Dimont, "To the Jews of Europe, this recognition of their own inherent power [of self-determination] over rabbis came as a shock."

Jewish emancipation during this time period was a two-stage process, as Jews needed to be emancipated both from within as well as without. Napoleon proved that he was willing to tear down the physical walls of the ghettoes, and the Jewish leaders then made the determination to deconstruct the psychological barriers that had existed ever since the diaspora began.

Jewish leaders had long stewarded their flock through an often-hostile world in which they had to remain separate and on their guard as a matter of sheer survival. They were now taking the bold step of setting their charges free. Emancipation had arrived. The Jews under

French dominion now felt free to mingle with their fellow non-Jewish citizens and work alongside them for the betterment of society.

In another interesting twist, Napoleon sanctioned the creation of a restored Sanhedrin. In ancient times, the Sanhedrin was the Jewish version of a supreme court. This was the first time that such an institution had existed since it was abolished by the Romans nearly 1,800 years prior. Although the Jews were, of course, ultimately under the authority of Napoleon's French Empire—a fact that was readily affirmed during the meeting—the symbolism alone of such an institution being restored sent shockwaves throughout the Jewish community. As Max Dimont put it, "For West European Jews, the affirmation of the Sanhedrin was a blast of the shofar that toppled the walls of their ghettos."

Napoleon was pleased too, as he had managed to break up potential focal points of resistance to his empire and instead brought them directly under his allegiance. In fact, Napoleon was so happy that he had a "commemorative coin" created in recognition of the event, in which Napoleon himself is depicted as a kind of "imperial Moses in regal robes" officiating the occasion.

Humility was certainly never Napoleon's strong suit. Nevertheless, despite all of his hubris, in 1815, Napoleon faced his final defeat at Waterloo, and the French Empire was no more. However, the Jewish emancipation that it helped to ignite would continue to unfold. In particular, the reforms that had started in France began to work their way across the Rhine into Germany. Soon, congregations in Berlin were implementing changes in how they conducted themselves. Instead of Hebrew, the congregation spoke the local language of German. Services were also moved to Sunday instead of Saturday, and previous restrictions on working during Shabbat (also known as the Sabbath) were removed. Most importantly, they placed ethics over dogmatic rituals and traditions.

The German reformers were pivotal to this transformation of the Jewish faith, but it was when they began immigrating to America that they really started revolutionizing Judaism. By the late 1800s, Reform Judaism was, by far, the most dominant form of Judaism in the United States of America, and today, it comprises the second-largest branch of Judaism on the planet.

The emancipation of the Jews required several steps in order to come to fruition. And some of the most important ones came from within the Jewish community itself.

Chapter 13: Looking toward Zion

"The Jewish question exists wherever the Jews live, however small their number. Where it does not exist it is imported by Jew immigrants. We naturally go where we are not persecuted, and, still persecution is the result of our appearance. By persecution we cannot be exterminated. The strong Jews turn proudly to their race when persecution bursts out. Entire branches of Judaism may disappear, break away; the tree lives."

—Theodor Herzl

As the 1800s gave way to the 1900s, imperialism was on the march. The sun never set on the British Empire, and France had colonies as far-flung as Vietnam. Japan, too, was cobbling together an empire in the Pacific, even though the United States was attempting to assert its dominance in the field. Meanwhile, the German-speaking world consisted of the two great central powers of Germany and the Austro-Hungarian Empire. The Russian Empire of eastern Europe/Eurasia and the Ottoman Empire of the Middle East made up much of the rest.

The world was split up into various conglomerates, which were held together more by a desire for an empire than anything else. This world of imperialism would be shaken to its core when, in 1914, a young Bosnian assassinated the heir-presumptive to the Austro-Hungarian throne, Franz Ferdinand, and his wife while they were visiting the city of Sarajevo. It was a localized event that would have repercussions on a global scale. Austro-Hungary ended up declaring war on Serbia, Russia declared war on Austro-Hungary, Germany declared war on Russia, and Britain and France declared war on Germany. This escalation continued until virtually the entire planet was at war with each other.

The Jewish diaspora was affected by the outbreak of World War One in a multitude of ways. In eastern Europe, the heavy concentration of Jewish communities was directly affected due to the massive onslaught of fighting waged between Russia and the forces of Germany and Austria. Poland, in particular, greatly suffered since it was, at that time, a part of the Russian Empire. But perhaps it was in Russia that the Jews suffered the most.

Even before the war, Tsar Nicholas II had been leading the nation into ruin. The Russian economy was tanking, and discord was quite common in the streets. In 1905, a massive protest was staged at the Winter Palace, with average everyday Russians attempting to get the attention of their ruler. The people believed the tsar was simply too detached and that he didn't know or understand what they were going through. They thought that if they could only reach him and make him aware, he would attempt to alleviate the problems of the average Russian.

But rather than show any sympathy or understanding, the tsar called in troops, which actually opened fire on the crowd, dispersing them through blood and bullets. The regime of Tsar Nicholas then tried to flip the script by pushing the buttons of anti-Semitism in an attempt to scapegoat the Jews for the problems of Russian society. The tsar's secret police, the Okhrana, actually incited the Russians to engage in violence against the Jewish population as a means to distract them from their real troubles.

This led to widespread persecution in Russia, and even when the police bothered to arrest those Russian nationals who attacked Jewish residents, the tsar usually granted the abusers clemency. But most saw through this ruse. They knew that the problems they faced were not the fault of Jewish Russians—it was the fault of those in charge. It was in this wretched, vicious, and vindictive state that the Russian Empire came tottering into World War One.

Russia, although much larger and more populous than its enemies, proved that it was about as ill-prepared as it could be. And once the fighting took a turn for the worse, with the Germans on the verge of defeating the Russian giant, an internal revolution in 1917 transformed the Russian Empire into what would become the communist-run Soviet Union.

Many have since, and to this day still, allege that the communists in Russia had a prominent Jewish influence. But this is simply not true. The only prominent Jewish figure in the Russian Revolution was Leon Trotsky, and he was later ostracized and exiled from the rest of the Russian communists, who were most certainly not Jews. In reality, much of the conspiracy regarding Jews and communism stems from the simple fact that the man who created communism—Karl Marx—was Jewish. Marx was indeed born a Jew, but it really doesn't mean anything. Just because the father of communism was Jewish does not mean he had a Jewish following. On the contrary, most of Karl Marx's followers were non-Jewish in origin. And even though Marx himself may have been Jewish in origin, he was certainly not a practicing Jew. Marx ridiculed Judaism and was an avowed atheist. In turn, most Jews of his day (Marx lived in the 1800s) disavowed him.

At any rate, like usual, the Jews suffered the most in the upheaval of the Russian Revolution. It seemed that in Russian society at this time, the Jews were often caught in the crosshairs of suspicion on multiple sides. According to one contemporary, the Jews were persecuted "by the Poles because they were Bolsheviks [and] by the Bolsheviks because they were not." In other words, each side of the ideological struggle viewed the Jew as the "other" and treated them terribly as a result. The Jews were inevitably viewed as the alien and outsider, and they were accused of stirring up plots and conspiracies against the societies in which they lived.

When Germany finally lost World War One, the same sad sentiments arose in Germans, who somehow felt that the Jews were responsible for their loss. Kaiser Wilhelm II himself was known to have made the remark that Germany had received a "stab in the back by Jews and profiteers." He and those like him seemed to think that there was some sort of Jewish cabal behind the war, one that somehow profited from the bloodshed.

But in reality, the Jews of Germany served in the armed forces as valiantly and patriotically as any other Germans did during the war. Nevertheless, the seeds of anti-Semitism were sown. And it was shortly after World War One came to a close that an unemployed, disillusioned veteran from the Western Front by the name of Adolph Hitler began trumpeting his own antisemitic beliefs to all who would listen to him. He, too, parroted the Kaiser's view that it was the Jews who had somehow weakened Germany and allowed for their disastrous defeat in the war. However, Hitler took his anti-Semitism even further by openly advocating the rooting out of all Jews from German society.

Many Jews in the diaspora were sensing just how precarious their situation was, and even though numerous Jews were doing generally well in places like Europe and the United States, there was a great sense of vulnerability due to the lack of a proper homeland for the Jewish people. Even before the war, a popular movement called Zionism had emerged among some members of the diaspora, which advocated a concerted effort to get the Jews back to their Jewish homeland of Israel. The term "Zionism" comes from "Zion," a Hebrew name for the city of Jerusalem. The founder of Zionism was an Austrian Jew by the name of Theodor Herzl. Due to increasing instances of anti-Semitism in Europe, Herzl was absolutely convinced that the Jewish people would not be safe until they had a homeland to call their own.

Herzl launched the First Zionist Congress in 1897, in which he and his fellow colleagues discussed the possibilities of a future Jewish state. Just a few years later, on May 17th, 1901, Herzl paid a visit to the Ottoman Empire to speak with Sultan Abdul Hamid II about the prospects of creating a Jewish state in Palestine. Herzl offered to have his Zionists raise money to alleviate some of the Ottomans' rising foreign debt in exchange for the deal. But the sultan was not too thrilled with the proposal.

In 1903, Herzl attempted to broker a deal with another power player on the world stage, Pope Pius X. However, the Vatican maintained that it was the policy of the Catholic Church that the Jews should not be allowed to return to the Holy Land as long as they "denied the divinity of Christ." It remains unclear how much the Vatican could have actually aided Herzl and his colleague even if they had wanted to, but this rejection must have been hard to take all the same. It's interesting to note the position that the Catholic Church took at the time since most Christians today would have one believe that Israel becoming a state fulfilled what was written in the scripture rather than denied it.

Herzl passed away in 1904 without his dream being fulfilled, but his compatriots carried on. In the aftermath of Theodore Herzl's death, the debate continued over just how Jews could gain greater access to Palestine. Immigrants had been slowly trickling in for decades, buying land from locals who often overcharged them, but such meager gains were no way to create a nation. Something big had to happen in order for a massive influx of Jewish immigrants to be possible.

The real game-changer for the Zionist cause occurred after World War One with the breakup of the Ottoman Empire. For 500 some years, the Muslim Ottoman Empire had controlled the land of Israel/Palestine. The Ottomans, whose seat of power rested in what we now call modern-day Turkey, at one time had a vast empire that controlled the whole of the Middle East and North Africa. However, the Ottomans chose the losing side of the war, as they joined forces with Germany and Austro-Hungary, and they paid the price as a result.

The Ottoman Empire died, and its corpse was dismembered. After its fall, the British took control of the region, which was then known as the British Mandate of Palestine. It was up to the British to figure out what to do with this territory, one that meant so much to the three main monotheistic faiths on the planet: Islam, Christianity, and Judaism.

The Zionists were quite successful in lobbying the British government, and in 1917, British Foreign Secretary Arthur James Balfour made a solemn declaration of British support for a "Jewish home in Palestine." To be clear, although they were a minority, Jews were already living in Palestine at the time. Independent Jewish immigration had picked up since the 1800s, with an estimated 75,000 making the move to Palestine from 1882 to 1914.

After the end of World War One, immigration to the British Mandate of Palestine picked up dramatically. After the war, the Twelfth Zionist Congress was held in 1921, in which postwar plans were actively discussed for what was now the British Mandate of Palestine. Among the primary concerns talked about was the status of Jewish-Arab relations. This dialogue resulted in the Congress passing "a proposal for an Arab-Jewish entente" to "forge a true understanding with the Arab nation."

As Jewish immigration picked up in Palestine in the 1920s, Jewish and Arab relations were fairly good at first. However, slowly but surely, a sense of Palestinian and Arab nationalism began to take hold, which rejected any notion of a Jewish claim to the Holy Land. This nationalism soon led to the resentment of the Jews before evolving into outright anti-Jewish demonstrations.

These demonstrations would erupt in a horrific fashion in the so-called "Arab riots" of 1929. The riots seemed to erupt spontaneously and lasted from August 23rd to August 29th. During the course of these protests, Jews were systematically attacked, and their property was destroyed in what could only be described as the Arab version of the German *Kristallnacht* ("Night of Broken Glass"). Jewish residents were forced to flee for their lives, and those who were not able to flee were killed. In total, 133 Jews were killed before the rioting had ceased. During the course of the conflict, about 116 Arabs were killed as well, primarily by British authorities attempting to stop the violence.

All in all, seventeen Jewish settlements had to be evacuated outright. It was certainly a terrible sight, and certainly not what many Jewish immigrants were expecting upon their arrival to their ancestral homeland. They wanted Israel/Palestine to be a peaceful refuge, not a place of violence. Nevertheless, after Hitler's Nazi Party came to power in Germany in 1933, for many Jews, the call to go back to Israel/Palestine grew even stronger.

Meanwhile, the British were having second thoughts. Despite previous pledges to secure a homeland in Palestine for the Jews, the British were taken aback by the vehement Arab resentment that had erupted. As such, they began to go back on their bargain and tried to work out the restriction of Jewish immigration while appeasing Arab residents. This resulted in the so-called "White Paper of 1939," which was introduced by the British government. It stated the intention to "reduce Jewish immigration to 15,000 a year for five years and then stop it altogether, aiming at freezing the Jews into a permanent minority" in Palestine. For Jews who wanted to create a Jewish state, being forced into a "permanent minority" status was certainly not what they had planned.

Shortly after this statement of Jewish settlement in Palestine had been issued, World War Two broke out. Almost immediately, the Arabs, who harbored hatred against the Jews, began to side with Hitler and the Axis Powers. It's an uncomfortable truth that many do not like bringing up, but Palestinian Arabs did indeed support the Nazis. The leader of the Palestinians, the so-called "Grand Mufti" Mohammed Amin al-Husseini, actually went to Germany and personally met Hitler himself. During their conference, the Nazis were considering the "Jewish question" in Europe, and they supposedly asked the Grand Mufti for advice. When the Palestinian leader was asked, "What should we do with the Jews?" the Grand Mufti is said to have coldly replied, "Burn them."

Now, this is not to suggest that the Grand Mufti of Palestine inspired the Nazis to commit the Holocaust, but at the same time, the outright hatred demonstrated by the Grand Mufti during this exchange cannot be denied. Prime Minister Benjamin Netanyahu of Israel courted controversy in 2015 when he claimed that the Grand Mufti was instrumental in the Holocaust. Netanyahu gave a speech at the World Zionist Congress that year in which he stated, "Hitler didn't want to exterminate the Jews at the time—he wanted to expel the Jews. And [then] Amin al-Husseini went to Hitler and said: 'If you expel them, they'll all come here.' 'So what should I do with them?' [Hitler] asked. [Husseini] said: 'Burn them'"

However, most historians would disagree with the idea that the fate of European Jews was decided with those two words. It is generally believed that the insidious "final solution" that the Germans came up with had already been decided before Hitler met the Grand Mufti and that their meeting was more or less for propaganda purposes. The Grand Mufti would later live in Germany toward the end of the war, and he would indeed become a chief propagandist, which the Nazis used as a recruitment tool for Muslims in places like Yugoslavia to entice the locals to join Nazi troops on the Eastern Front.

Benjamin Netanyahu, who is Jewish, was roundly condemned for the suggestion, and his opposition leader in Israel, Isaac Herzog, went so far as to declare, "This is a dangerous historical distortion and I demand Netanyahu correct it immediately as it minimizes the Holocaust, Nazism and Hitler's part in our people's terrible disaster."

The horror of the Holocaust was officially sanctioned by the Nazi regime on January 20th, 1942, at the Wannsee Conference, which took place on the outskirts of Berlin. The meeting was headed by Reinhard Heydrich, who introduced a plot to move Jews en masse to concentration camps that had just been established in recently conquered and German-occupied Poland. The first known mass killing via gas then occurred at "camp Belzec" outside the town of Lublin on March 17th.

As planned, Poland became the site of several death camps, which would include Sobibor, Treblinka, Chełmno, Majdanek, and, of course, the infamous Auschwitz. Jews, in addition to other minority groups, were sent to these camps. The largest group to be brought to the death camps in one sitting occurred in late 1942 when 300,000 Jews were taken from the Warsaw Ghetto and sent to the death camps. By the end of the war in 1945, it is estimated that around six million Jews had perished in concentration camps. The Germans tried to cover up their crimes, but as one could imagine, the murder of six million people is not something one can easily hide.

Nevertheless, when reports began to be leaked to Allied intelligence as to what was happening in Nazi-occupied territory, many didn't believe it. The accounts just sounded too terrible to believe. Many felt that surely the tales of genocide were an exaggeration and that surely an advanced European state like Germany would not engage in the systematic liquidation of an entire people group. But sadly, the reports were not exaggerated, and toward the end of the war, when the Allies began to liberate the camps, they saw the horrors that had been inflicted on minority groups with their own eyes.

It still boggles the mind to come to grips with how such a thing could take place. How could a civilized, modern society allow such terrible things to occur? At the war crimes tribunal in Nuremberg, most said that they were simply following orders. Edmund Burke, an Irish philosopher who lived in the 1700s, once said, "The only thing necessary for the triumph of evil is for good men to do nothing." The Holocaust would seem to lend credence to that notion because very few spoke out against what was happening in Germany at the time.

Although the Holocaust was ordered in 1942, it actually took place in several stages. First, the Jews were politically and economically marginalized, then herded into various prison camps and ghettos. After this, the death camps were set up, where the Jews were shipped en masse. The death camps were disguised as labor camps, and the Jews were indeed forced to work at the facilities. Disconnected from friends, family, and hope, inmates were forced to toil away in a never-ending nightmare. At Auschwitz, they were greeted with the infamous words of "Arbeit Macht Frei!" which were engraved into the gates. In English, this translates as "Work makes you free!" This was yet another ironic cruelty foisted upon the inmates because the Nazis knew that the only way the Jews would gain freedom was through death. For those who were not literally worked to death, they would end up meeting the Nazi quota for liquidation and be gassed in carefully calculated groups.

Although surely some must have suspected it, none were told what was going to happen to them. The Nazis were so insidious that they created gas chambers with the façade of being public showers. They would have Jews separated by gender and then sent to the "showers," telling them it was simply a routine procedure to disinfect them from potential parasites. But when the Nazis flipped the switch, rather than water coming out of the shower nozzle, poisonous gas poured out. Only at the very end, as they gasped for air, did many understand what was actually happening to them.

The madness only ended when the Soviets managed to rally their strength and push the Germans out of Poland. In fact, it was the Soviet Union who liberated Auschwitz in January of 1945. Soviet troops would later recall the eerie feeling of stepping into the compound that the Nazis had just abandoned moments before. Initially, they thought the complex was empty, but after a cursory check of the premises, they were astonished to find thousands of emaciated Jews—survivors of the Holocaust—still in the camp. One Soviet soldier who was there that day, a man named Georgi Elisavetski, would remember that moment for the rest of his life. He would forever recall the reactions of the skin and bone survivors when they realized that they were truly free from the horrors that had been inflicted upon them. According to Georgi, "They rushed toward us shouting, fell on their knees, kissed the flaps of our overcoats, and threw their arms around our legs."

Shortly after the Soviets liberated Auschwitz, they moved on to liberate the killing facilities of Treblinka, Sobibor, and Belzec. Allied troops also stumbled upon and liberated the wretched death camps of Dachau, Mauthausen, Buchenwald, Dora-Mittelbau, Flossenbürg, Neuengamme, and Bergen-Belsen. In all, these death camps would claim the lives of an estimated six million Jews, as well as over eleven million deaths of other minority groups. According to Martin Gilbert, a British historian, this number represented about one-third of the world's Jews. Nevertheless, it was from the ashes of the terrible Holocaust that a new nation would be born.

Chapter 14: The Creation of the Modern State of Israel

"It all happened so fast. The ghetto. The deportation. The sealed cattle car. The fiery altar upon which the history of our people and the future of mankind were meant to be sacrificed."

—Elie Wiesel

The early Zionists of the late 19th and early 20th centuries had long argued that the Jews would never be safe unless their own homeland was established. The Holocaust, of course, seemed to prove in dramatic fashion just how right those assertions were.

Immediately before the outbreak of World War Two, the British, who were controlling the so-called "British Mandate of Palestine," had severely restricted Jewish immigration to Israel. But even after the war and the horrors of the Holocaust had been revealed to the world, the British still dithered in their commitment to the founding of a Jewish nation. It was soon apparent to Jewish leaders that they would have to force the issue themselves. And soon, in defiance of the Brits' so-called "White Paper" that restricted their access, the Jews of Europe, many of them Holocaust survivors, began to charter their own vessels to sail "through illegal channels" to British-controlled Palestine.

With this fresh influx of Jews, the Arabs again reacted with violence, but the Jews who had just survived World War Two and the Holocaust were more than ready to fight back, and they ferociously returned every blow they were dealt. For many, the creation of a Jewish state was viewed as a clear necessity to survival, and they were not going to back down. For them, it was all or nothing.

Matters came to a head in 1947 when, due to the growing chaos that had erupted, the British finally made an appeal to the newly established United Nations to take the troubling matter off their hands. The United Nations sent in a team of experts to investigate what was going on, and after six months of looking into the matter, they recommended a "partition of Palestine into a Jewish state, and an Arab state, with Jerusalem as an international city."

In November of 1947, the UN voted for the partition of Palestine to proceed, with the Soviet Union and the United States backing the determination. With this in the works, the British then announced that they would leave the region by May of 1948. The Jewish settlers, meanwhile, made their plans clear in announcing their independence even though Arab leaders declared they would "drive the Jews into the sea."

It was on the heels of these events that the so-called "Palestinian Exodus" began. The causes of the Palestinian Exodus are still a matter of intense debate on both sides of the conflict. Official sources are still not certain whether the Palestinians were expelled or left of their own accord; it is also very possible that it was a combination of both factors. However, the fact remains that in the month of May, in the lead-up to Israel's declaration of statehood in 1948, some 750,000 Palestinians left their homes, crossing over into Arab-controlled territory.

The pro-Israel side of this debate insists that the Jews had nothing to do with the Palestinians leaving. In fact, they claim that efforts were made to convince them to stay. This side of the debate makes the assertion that Arab leaders "ordered" Palestinian civilians to "leave the field" in order to clear the way for Arab armies to assault Israeli positions without any hindrance. It has also been suggested that the Palestinians simply did not want to live under a Jewish-controlled government, and as such, they left as soon as Israel's statehood was declared.

According to this theory, Arab leaders promised the Palestinians they could return to their homes as soon as the Jewish forces were defeated. Those who believe this version of events maintain that the refugee crisis was therefore created when the Arab leaders, who were certain that Israel would be "driven into the sea," were defeated, rendering them unable to deliver on their promises.

However, many Palestinians insist that the reason they fled was because of Israeli aggression. It has been claimed that even before Israel's 1948 declaration of statehood, Israeli paramilitary groups were systematically driving Palestinians out of the land. Israel denies this ever occurred. All of this, of course, is still hotly debated between both sides of the conflict, and as of right now, we don't know the full truth. The fact still remains that the Palestinians, who had lived in the region for centuries, left the only home they ever knew (much like the Jews back in the day), and many are still displaced today. Over half of those who live outside what once comprised Palestine are stateless, meaning they have no citizenship in any country. The Palestinians have been calling for the "right of return," which, as the name suggests, calls for the Palestinians to take back their land. This will more than likely play a major factor in any potential future peace agreement between Israel and Palestine.

On May 14th, 1948, Jewish statesman and the later prime minister David Ben-Gurion announced the statehood of Israel. Just a few hours later, the president of the United States, Harry S. Truman, then officially recognized the new state of Israel, making the United States the first country to do so. However, the very day that Israel's statehood was declared, armies from neighboring Arab countries were on the march. Egypt, Jordan, Syria, and Lebanon struck Israel from all sides, threatening to make good on their threat of driving the newfound Israelis into the sea.

Beyond all odds, the outnumbered and surrounded Jews were able to mount a counteroffensive that stopped the Jordanians, who had poured into Jerusalem from the east, and halted the Egyptians, who were advancing through the south. The Syrians, meanwhile, were utterly decimated, and the Lebanese were forced back into Lebanon. It was at this point, right when Israel was poised to make even more territorial gains, that the United Nations came in and brokered a truce.

At the cessation of the conflict, Israel was stronger than ever. The only real victory on the Arab side was the fact that Jordan managed to hang onto the West Bank, which it officially annexed in 1950. Jordan would ultimately give up the territory after its disastrous defeat in the Six-Day War.

The Six-Day War occurred in 1967, and it lasted from June 5th until June 10th—literally six days. In this conflict, Israel was once again fought against a multitude of Arab nations. The main players were Egypt, Syria, and Jordan, with Iraq and Lebanon providing some additional support. Once again, Israel smashed all of its opponents, doing so in record time. This victory allowed Israel to gain limited control of the West Bank and the Gaza Strip.

This war would lead to another one, as the Arab nations tried to wrest the territory back. This new conflict was known as the Yom Kippur War, named this because it began during the Jewish holiday of the same name, and it began in 1973. The war began when Egyptian and Syrian armies launched a simultaneous attack through both the Sinai Peninsula in the south and from the Golan Heights to Israel's north. Israel managed to hold back the Egyptians, but the Syrians had some early successes in battle. The Israelis managed to rally, and after a few days, they pushed the Syrians all the way back to the Syrian capital of Damascus. They then managed to push the Egyptians all the way back to the Egyptian city of Suez.

It was at this point that the United Nations stepped in once again and managed to broker yet another ceasefire. Fortunately, this would be the last war that Israel would have to wage against Egypt. Just a few years later, on March 26th, 1979, with the help of US President Jimmy Carter, Israel and Egypt normalized relations, making Egypt the first Muslim country to recognize Israel.

Nearly two decades later, Jordan decided to follow suit, signing a peace treaty with Israel in 1994 under the stewardship of US President Bill Clinton. This meant that two of the main aggressors in Israel's past were officially at peace with the nation before the 20th century came to a close.

The next Arab nations that would come to the table were the United Arab Emirates (UAE), Bahrain, Sudan, and Morocco. In 2020, under the presidency of Donald Trump, all four of these nations decided to normalize their relations with Israel, one after the other.

Despite what anyone might try to tell you, this is big news. In 1948, there were no Muslim majority countries willing to acknowledge Israel's right to exist. Now, Egypt, Jordan, the UAE, Bahrain, Sudan, and Morocco have all agreed to not only recognize Israel but also become trading partners with the Jewish state. Instead of wanting to fight with Israel, these nations are wanting to do business. One can only hope that this trend of peace will continue for the sake of the Jews, Israel, and the whole world.

Conclusion: The Story of the World

The Jews arose from obscurity in the Middle East. The children of Israel then found themselves in the land of Canaan—their Promised Land—before being diverted to Egypt. There, they languished in slavery for a few centuries until a leader named Moses rose up to lead them to freedom. The hope of an entire nation rested upon his fortuitous yet reluctant shoulders.

Scripture tells us that Moses lacked confidence in his mission from the beginning and that he even questioned God when told of his divine commission. He was certainly not a perfect leader, yet he was the one who was chosen for the task. He repeatedly stumbled and fumbled. He even had a bad case of stage fright when he had to speak in front of the Egyptian pharaoh. Yet, nevertheless, Moses led his people back to the land that they were promised.

Once free from the bonds of Egypt, Israel was initially ruled by a series of judges, who were selected for their shrewd ability to size up the situation and provide the nation just what it needed at just the right time. Eventually, however, the Jews longed to have a king like their neighbors.

The children of Israel were warned not to seek out or covet such cultural conventionalities, but the push for a potentate among the populace soon proved inevitable. This desire brought them a long line of kings, some good, some bad. It brought them King David, but it also brought them King Herod—and, of course, all of the plotting and dynastic intrigue that lay between.

In the meantime, foreign powers rose up all around the Jewish state, and they began to interfere with Israel's destiny. The kingdom was split apart and invaded, and the whole of Judea was eventually sent into the Babylonian captivity. However, they would return to rebuild their nation. But Israel would yet again come under the dominion of another foreign power, first the Greeks, then the Romans.

The Romans would tear down their temple and eject the Jews into a diaspora that would last nearly 2,000 years. A lot of things happened between then and the founding of modern-day Israel in 1948. The land of Zion rose and fell, then rose again. They were knocked down, but no matter what happened, they always got back up. Whole empires have bitten the dust long ago, but Israel remains. The story of the Jews is one of struggle, determination, and victory. The story of the Jews is the story of the entire world.

Here's another book by Captivating History that you might like

Free Bonus from Captivating History (Available for a Limited time)

Hi History Lovers!

Now you have a chance to join our exclusive history list so you can get your first history ebook for free as well as discounts and a potential to get more history books for free! Simply visit the link below to join.

Captivatinghistory.com/ebook

Also, make sure to follow us on Facebook, Twitter and Youtube by searching for Captivating History.

Appendix A: Further Reading and Reference

Everyman's History of the Jews. Sulamith Ish-Kishor, 2018.

A Short History of the Jewish People: From Legendary Times to Modern Statehood. Raymond P. Scheindlin, 2000.

A History of the Jews: The Indestructible Jews, The Jews in America, and Appointment in Jerusalem. Max I. Dimont, 2017.

A History of the Jewish People. Abraham Malamat, 1976.

Jensen's Survey of the Old Testament. Irving L. Jensen, 1978.

Jensen's Survey of the New Testament. Irving L. Jensen, 1981.

The Great Roman-Jewish War. Flavius Josephus, 2012.

Printed in the USA
CPSIA information can be obtained
at www.ICGtesting.com
LVHW021504210923
758784LV00021B/39